Teaching with Books

TEACHING
WITH BOOKS

A STUDY OF
COLLEGE LIBRARIES

BY

HARVIE BRANSCOMB

DIRECTOR OF LIBRARIES
DUKE UNIVERSITY

ASSOCIATION OF
AMERICAN COLLEGES

AMERICAN LIBRARY
ASSOCIATION
CHICAGO

1940

This publication was made possible by funds granted by Carnegie Corporation of New York. That Corporation is not, however, the author, owner, publisher, or proprietor of this publication, and is not to be understood as approving by virtue of its grant any of the statements made or views expressed therein.

This Book Is Dedicated to

FREDERICK PAUL KEPPEL

ONCE A COLLEGE DEAN,

NOW HEAD OF

A GREAT PHILANTHROPIC TRUST,

YET ALWAYS A TEACHER OF AMERICAN YOUTH

THROUGH COLLEGE LIBRARIES

WHOSE EFFECTIVENESS AND RESOURCES

HE HAS SO NOTABLY ADVANCED

Foreword

THE OFFICERS OF THE ASSOCIATION OF AMERICAN COL-
leges have felt for some years that the college library
needs to be coordinated more effectively with the educational and recreational programs of the college.
There needs to be a development of more interest in
library administration on the part of members of the
teaching and administrative staffs. The library staff
needs to develop a better understanding and more interest in the educational program of the college. The
library should be organized, housed, and administered
in the best possible way so as to be considered by trustees, faculty, officers, and students alike as indispensable a feature of the educational and recreational programs of the college as the laboratory is to the program
of the science departments. To come to some positive
and constructive conclusions about this problem, the
Association organized in the spring of 1937 a study
known as The Library Project.

"Teaching with Books" is the outcome of this Library Project of the Association of American Colleges
made possible by a grant from the Carnegie Corporation. Dr. Harvie Branscomb was quite a logical
choice as the director of this project. He was pecu-
liarly fitted for the task assigned, not only because of
his position as Director of Libraries and Professor of
early Christian Literature at Duke University, and his
experience in organizing and directing the large library collections there, but also because of his undergraduate and postgraduate study at Birmingham-

Southern College, Oxford University (on a Rhodes Scholarship), and Columbia University. During the college year 1937-38, he maintained an office at the headquarters of the Association.

In preparation for the book, Dr. Branscomb visited college and university libraries in all sections of the nation. He conferred with college administrators and librarians and others who have been conspicuous in their study and writings in the college library field. He participated in a number of conferences and college association meetings. The result of his work should advance the better correlation of the college library in the teaching process of the liberal arts college.

GUY E. SNAVELY

Preface

WHEN THE OFFICERS OF THE ASSOCIATION OF AMERICAN
Colleges asked me to make a year's study of American
college libraries, the first task was to clarify the subject
of the investigation. There were several possible inter-
pretations of the commission, any one of which might
have led to the initiation of useful and important
projects. One line of research would have involved a
factual survey of the status and condition of the libraries which would have resulted in a statistical summary
of their holdings, expenditures and general condition
of development. Such a survey would have been valuable, but it was believed that a compendium of this
sort might be more appropriately and effectively prepared by other agencies. Nor was it felt that a manual
of college library administration was the desired goal.
The task which the directors approved and which I
undertook was rather a consideration of the extent to
which the efforts of the college library are integrated
with those of the institution as a whole. In other
words, this project undertook to study the college library from the standpoint of its educational effectiveness rather than its administrative efficiency. To this
end several local studies were set up, some 60 college
libraries visited, many librarians and college presidents interviewed, and the immediate data thus secured supplemented by constant use of the published
literature in the field.

A volume on this theme is addressed, of course, to
college presidents, teachers, librarians and others re-

sponsible for undergraduate education. The point of
view and the problems of the first group, however,
have been especially in mind, and it is hoped that the
book may to some degree interpret the college library
to college presidents, particularly those whose previous
experience has not been in academic fields. This fact
explains in part the choice of topics discussed. The
criticism was made by one person who read the manuscript that certain of the later chapters contain nothing new to professional librarians who have kept up
with the literature of their field. The book is designed,
however, for a somewhat wider group of readers. College presidents, similarly, who are familiar with the
newer programs of college instruction may regard the
discussion of these matters as repetitious and unnecessary. These difficulties will be forgiven by those who
believe that on occasion at least the pattern, technique,
and even vocabulary of the educational specialist are
to be abhorred, and also that problems of library use
are a common responsibility of the whole academic
body.

It will be fairly obvious to one who reads the volume that the obligations of the writer are multitudi-
nous. Were I to attempt to enumerate the librarians
and college presidents to whom I am indebted for information and ideas, the remainder of the volume
would tend to take on the appearance of an appendix.
The only proper preface for the pages which follow
would be the lines,

> You ask me for something original.
> I scarcely know where to begin,
> For I possess nothing original,
> Excepting original sin.

Advance information is to the effect that a good many
librarians will subscribe to the accuracy of both affir-
mations in the stanza.

Preface

I must be content thus with a general expression of indebtedness and thanks. To certain individuals I cannot forego a special word of gratitude. Dr. Guy E. Snavely, Executive Secretary of the Association of American Colleges, has been of such assistance that the volume would not be complete without this acknowledgment. Besides aid in innumerable practical matters, he has combined a perfect balance of suggestion and counsel with complete freedom to the Author to develop the study along his own lines. Nor can I leave unmentioned a special debt to President Wriston of Brown University. I believe it was his idea in the first place that such a study should be made. Not only has he been more than generous in his interest in the study, but the writer remembers with special gratefulness one snowy evening in New York when, seated on the floor with his back to the radiator, he definitely rescued the project from danger of bogging down in a morass of alternative possibilities. A third individual who has placed me permanently in his debt is Mr. Robert M. Lester, Secretary of the Carnegie Corporation. He has been untiring in his assistance, making available data from the files of the Corporation, suggesting sources of information, and giving to the undertaking the same critical interest for which so many other students of library matters have had occasion to be grateful.

Dr. Carl M. White and Dr. John J. Lund have read all or portions of the manuscript and made valuable suggestions. To the members of Committee "S" of the American Association of University Professors and especially to its chairman, Dr. Van Hoesen, I am grateful for meeting with me to discuss certain of the topics under investigation. Most especially my thanks are due Miss Anne Strowd, who has been associated with the project from its beginning, prepared much of the data, and made many suggestions for the prosecution of the study and its improvement.

H. B.

Durham, N. C.

Contents

List of Tables

List of Tables

List of Tables

Teaching with Books

CHAPTER ONE

The Problem of the
College Library

THE MOST IMPRESSIVE FACT ABOUT UNIVERSITY AND COL-
lege libraries in recent years has been their amazing
growth. In 1900 the Harvard Library contained 560,-
000 volumes; in 1938, approximately 4,000,000. The
Yale Library had 285,000 volumes in 1900 and over
2,500,000 in 1938. Columbia increased its library holdings from 295,000 volumes to over 1,500,000. Such
illustrations could be multiplied, though not all of
them, of course, in figures of such gargantuan proportions. The latest figures available for the holdings of
college, university and professional schools yield a
total of approximately 63,000,000 volumes,[1] and
annual expenditures for library purposes totaling
$14,894,852.[2] This wealth in books, like the national
wealth in general, is not of course evenly distributed.
The poor we have with us always. But these smaller
college libraries can boast also of impressive increases
in the size of their book collections.

Although it is generally recognized that this growth
has been phenomenal, it is difficult to determine what
it has been for the universities and colleges as a group.
The figure, if ascertained accurately, would probably
be meaningless anyhow. Mr. Carl White in a paper
read to the December 1937 meeting of the American
Library Association presented a table showing the
growth of fourteen university libraries which had kept

[1]U.S. Office of Education, *Biennial Survey of Education, 1934-36,*
Bulletin 1937, No.2 (Washington: Government Printing Office, 1938),
vol. II, ch. iv, p.21.
[2]*Ibid.,* p.42.

accurate and comparable records for a period of 25 years.[3] The total number of volumes in these libraries had increased during the period from 5,036,405 to 14,200,662, an increase of 281.9 per cent. The combined annual accessions of these libraries in 1912-13 totaled 227,385; in 1936-37 they were 590,400, an increase of 259.6 per cent.[4] In other words, the rate of growth has been so accelerated as to indicate a continuation of this increase. Total book expenditures of this group of libraries in 1936-37, omitting one for which the record was not complete, was 329.7 per cent of the figure 25 years earlier.[5] There is every reason for thinking that these figures are typical of what has been happening in the university and more substantial college libraries.

With these greatly increased book collections, increased annual accessions and larger expenditures, are there any grounds for speaking of a college library problem? Certainly no one could deprecate these increased educational facilities. Their acquisition has been a praiseworthy accomplishment, which offsets to some extent, perhaps, expenditures on intercollegiate athletics and other exuberances of the American college. A good book is a permanently valuable acquisition. A library, as has often been said, is a university in itself. It is also a great academic equalizer. Colleges not able to boast of faculties of distinction can possess nevertheless in their libraries the thought and major achievements of the best scholars and scientists of their generation. There is every reason to be proud of the growth of the college book collections.

The problem of the college libraries can be stated very simply. It is that of securing a sufficient use of

---

[3]Carl M. White, "Trends in the Use of University Libraries." A. F. Kuhlman, ed., *College and University Library Service* (Chicago: American Library Association, 1938), p.15-39.
[4]*Ibid.*, Table 3, p.22.
[5]*Ibid.*, Table 4, p.23.

these enlarged resources to justify the investment that has been and is being put into them. To this problem neither librarians nor college faculties for the most part have given a great deal of attention. In the developments of the last 25 years more emphasis has been placed on the acquisition and preservation of library materials than upon their use. The means have absorbed more attention than the ends. The libraries have expanded greatly, but the use of them by the undergraduates, on whose account primarily they were acquired, is in most institutions, as will be shown later, distinctly disconcerting. This central problem has several aspects depending upon the point of view from which it is considered.

1. As stated above, the last several decades have been for libraries a period characterized primarily by the acquisition of materials. Libraries have doubled and quadrupled in size. This accumulation created acute problems of organization of the materials secured. How should these books be grouped on the shelves? How should they be cataloged? Inevitably, the technical problems dominated the attention of librarians. One who doubts this need only look over the program of professional library meetings or leaf through the pages of the professional journals. To be good librarians those who held that title had first of all to be efficient technicians. Circumstances made it almost inevitable that they would be concerned with books rather than with students. It is easily understandable that some of the larger problems of the college, problems closely related to the task of teaching, should have been left largely to the attention of others.

2. The period of book accumulation has also been one in which librarianship has emerged as a profession. This is supposed to date from the founding of the American Library Association in 1876. The more important dates are probably those of the founding of the library schools. The first library school was that

5

at Columbia College, New York, founded by Melvil Dewey in 1887. The Pratt Institute School of Library Science was organized in 1890. It was not until 1915, however, that the Association of American Library Schools was organized with ten charter members. These schools, it must be remembered, were called into existence primarily to provide a personnel for the public library movement, which with Andrew Carnegie's aid was spreading so beneficently over the country. The training they provided was largely of a technical character. College libraries, which had been directed usually by a faculty member, were turned over to these trained library workers. Their services along technical and strictly professional lines do not need to be chronicled here. But along with the gains went corresponding losses. The professional librarians, equipped with specific training rather than general scholarship, were not qualified to take an active part in the discussion or execution of the educational program, and too often were given little opportunity to develop interests and capacities in this direction. A division of function was established which is still regulative: librarians were responsible for the care of books and faculty members for their use. Only in the field of recreational reading has the college library staff as a whole felt itself responsible for the use of the books in their buildings, a field in which, incidentally, a considerable carry-over of the experience and point of view of the public librarian can be plainly seen. Thus the previous training of librarians and the gap between the library staff and the faculty tended to accentuate the emphasis on technical processes which the condition and rapid growth of the libraries was in itself only too likely to initiate.

That this condition is not merely an historic interlude, but still obtains to greater or lesser degree, cannot be doubted by one who visits a considerable number of educational institutions. Mr. Randall, who knows college libraries as well or better than any man in the country, commenting on his survey of 205 institutions in connection with Carnegie Corporation grants, records his impression as follows:

> It is evident from conversation with the librarians of these colleges that the importance attached to the catalog is very great. . . .This and other facts all point to the conclusion that the approach to the problems of the college library has been sought primarily from the side of the books themselves rather than through a study of the users of the books. A great catalog, a careful classification, an accession book which shows at a glance the number of volumes in the library: these are the things to which college librarians point with pride. The task of bringing about a contact between the books and the students is left largely to the faculty of the institution and to the least mature and experienced members of the library staff.[6]

Other illustrations of this point of view will be encountered in the pages which follow. One of the most remarkable is the extent to which even in small libraries books have been separated from the students by closed stacks and closed reserves. As will be remarked later, this can be justified in part in the larger institutions and in smaller ones in certain special circumstances. For most colleges, however, no such necessity exists, and the practice reveals the extent to which the determinative principles have been the administration and care of books rather than the stimulation of student minds.

This division of function has been particularly unfortunate from the standpoint of the library staff, for it has tended to reduce their status to that of administrators, technicians and clerks. Librarians have invariably rebelled at the situation, but the present program seems to offer little means of escape. It will not

[6]William M. Randall, *The College Library* (Chicago: American Library Association and University of Chicago Press, 1932), p.54.

7

be until librarians begin to concern themselves with the effectiveness of the educational program that they will take their place as true colleagues of the teaching members of the college faculty.

3. Thus far the problem has been approached from the standpoint of the library staff. The credit for the enlargement of college and university book collections during the last few decades must go in large part to the faculties which have insisted on their need for more books. Nevertheless it becomes painfully apparent as one studies the situation that faculties as a whole have not learned how to make very effective use of the library in their teaching. The proof of this statement is the limited use which the majority of college students make of the library, of which more will be said later. The theory of the "library method" is eloquently upheld by all faculty groups, but the cold facts seem to be that a great many instructors are quite satisfied with a student performance defined in terms of the knowledge and wisdom expressed in the textbook and in class discussion. So plain is this general fact that the question must be raised whether we need these large libraries, if present teaching methods continue. Discussion has already broken out as to whether the college library of the future will not be a small book collection changing in content from time to time. This is, perhaps, the fundamental problem of the college library, namely, what is really needed for college work and how can it be most effectively used. Even a small contribution to this problem would justify much effort.

4. The necessity for a reconsideration of the library arises, on the other hand, from a quite different quarter, namely, the adoption by many institutions of methods of teaching which emphasize student responsibility and self-direction. Twenty-five years ago, when college teaching was largely done by class discussion, textbooks, and the uniform reading of certain col-

lateral assignments, the library problem of the college was relatively simple. It consisted, for the most part, of providing in sufficient numbers the collateral readings, along with, of course, certain reference tools and current periodicals. The reserve book room under such conditions was virtually the undergraduates' library. The deficiencies of this mode of instruction, however, have been rather completely revealed, certainly as regards the last two years of college work. If education means awakening rather than the acquisition of facts or views, and if the characteristics of the educated individual are inquisitiveness, independence and intellectual courage and initiative, the older method is not entirely satisfactory. Hence there have developed the various methods which throw an increasing responsibility upon the individual student—honors courses, comprehensive examinations, senior theses, and tutorial plans of one sort or the other. This increased freedom and responsibility means that teaching is transferred to a large extent from the classroom to the library. The book collection emerges more clearly than formerly as an instructional tool of the first importance, and the library as the place where a far larger share of the undergraduates' work will be done than used to be the case. Whatever may have been true heretofore, a library program which does not echo the educational objectives which the institution has defined will prove a definite obstacle to the achievement of these goals. The efforts of library staff and the faculty must be more closely coordinated, for the simple reason that it has become increasingly clear that their respective responsibilities do not merely overlap, but have merged.

5. To sum up, it may be said without hesitation that the fundamental need of the college library is to develop a distinctive program of its own. Absorbed as it has been in the task of increasing its supply of books and compelled to serve a constantly increasing student

body, paying small salaries and getting usually—though not always—no more than it paid for, it has been too imitative of other institutions. The public library, which has influenced so strongly the training of professional librarians, and the large university library have been its models. The architecture of most college libraries, for example, with the books kept in a darkened central stack, surrounded by a few carrels or desks, and with one or more reading rooms out front, is an imitation of research libraries. This plan represents an effort to make available a great collection of books to a relatively few research workers. The college problem is, however, exactly the opposite, to make available a smaller collection of books to a relatively large number of undergraduate students. A distinctive and functional form of college library architecture has yet to be evolved. The influence of the public library is to be seen in various ways. Theoretically, the college librarian does all the book selection, just as it is done in the public library. No very helpful program has been worked out as to just what the librarian should contribute to this task in view of the presence on the college campus of specialists in the various subject fields. The proper field of the reference librarian is equally vague and undefined. In the public library this official interprets the library to its users and aids people in finding desired information. How such service should be correlated with instructional assignments and the generally different situation in a college, certainly needs clarification. The catalog reflects a number of divergent influences. The addition of such details on the catalog cards as the number of preliminary pages, the size of the volume, the color of ink on title pages, or the copy number of books printed in limited editions seems to reflect the rare book tradition. In a college library where the book itself can be consulted in case of doubt, no elaborate details would seem to be necessary. Similarly, one might remark that the usual subject headings used in catalog making have had little criticism from the standpoint of their pertinency to college work.[7]

In these and many other details one sees the need of an appraisal of the college program in the light of its particular task. This latter is obvious enough, namely, to function as an integral part of the educational process for which the college exists.

The present study addresses itself to this problem. It is not alone in doing so. During the last year or so, considerable interest in this topic has developed. At the 1937 meeting of the American Library Association the Association of College and Reference Libraries was organized to give more adequate attention to the interests of these groups. In recent professional meetings a number of papers have been presented drawing attention to the need for a closer integration of the college library with the other educational forces on the campus. The present volume has the modest hope of adding to this developing discussion.

[7]See the article on "The University Library," by Gustave O. Arlt and John J. Lund in *Library Journal*, LXII (1937), 766ff. for a discussion of the university library's tendency to follow blindly public library methods and the "book collector tradition." Note also the comment of W. N. C. Carlton, "As a class college librarians have unquestionably not kept pace with the public [librarians]," "College Libraries and College Librarians," *Library Journal*, XXXI (1906), 751.

CHAPTER TWO

How Much do Undergraduates Use the Library?

THE USEFULNESS OR VALUE OF A COLLEGE LIBRARY CAN never be measured, for the library is an educational institution, and education, according to the best liberal arts tradition, is an awakening and a growth. Were it a matter of amassing a certain amount of factual information, one might conceive of some super-questionnaire which would ascertain the sources from which students obtain this learning. But who can measure the stimulating or awakening power of many aspects of library activity which can never be recorded —a visit to the periodical room with its display of intellectual interests in such variety, the perusal of an exhibit of rare manuscripts, or the examination of a shelf of new or ancient books? These things defy measurement. Nor can one estimate the value of enabling a student to read even one or two significant volumes which otherwise he would not have seen. The reading of one book has been known to change a life. Any complete estimate of the effectiveness of a library would involve these qualitative considerations, and makes any effort at determining the quantitative use of libraries seem a useless procedure.

Nevertheless it is obvious that libraries have a wide range of possible usefulness. Granting therefore the impossibility of any complete or absolute appraisal of the library's effectiveness, one cannot avoid the necessity of some effort at determining the extent to which the institution is performing its intended function.

If one asks how much students use their college and

university libraries, the first answer which the librarians will give will probably be, a great deal more than they used to. A questionnaire recently sent to a number of college librarians, for example, elicited from 88 per cent of those replying the statement that the use of the library had steadily increased.[1] Mr. Carl White has collected from university libraries an impressive body of statistics to prove the point. Individual libraries reported loans 6, 9, 12, and even 400 times the number in 1912. For 5 institutions he was able to get continuous and consistent circulation figures for a span of 23 years. The combined recorded circulation of these 5 libraries in 1936-37 was more than 5 times what it was in 1914-15. Continuous and consistent figures for a 10 year period were available from 23 university libraries. The combined circulation showed an increase from 7,774,426 loans in 1927-28 to 10,817,424 in 1936-37. This was an increase of 39.11 per cent.[2] That the increase is due, however, in considerable part to the simple fact of a largely increased student enrolment, is revealed by Mr. White's figures. During the 10 year period in the 23 libraries referred to above the total number of students and faculty members increased by 15.1 per cent. Translated into per capita terms the recorded circulation in these libraries showed an increase in the 10 years from 40.8 loans per capita to 48.41 loans. This is an increase of 20.7 per cent, or an average of about 2 per cent per year.[3]

[1] Leland R. Smith, "Trends in the Use of College Libraries...," A. F. Kuhlman, ed., *College and University Library Service* (Chicago: American Library Association, 1938), p.41.

[2] Carl M. White, "Trends in the Use of University Libraries," A. F. Kuhlman, ed., *College and University Library Service* (Chicago: American Library Association, 1938), p.15ff.

[3] *Ibid.*, Table 2, p.17. Mr. White secured his data directly from librarians and registrars of the institutions concerned. Such a tabulation involving over 10,000,000 withdrawals and nearly 250,000 individuals represents the most careful and thorough study of the subject which has been presented. Mr. White emphasizes that the value of the figures lies in their consistency from year to year. They afford therefore a statistically dependable basis for a year to year comparison, though not for comparisons between one institution and another.

This increase, which may be assumed to be fairly representative of the university libraries, is a source of satisfaction, but it is apparent that the greater activity which is so impressive to the librarian does not represent quite the increase in interest on the part of the individual student as has often been assumed. If one looks at the matter from the standpoint of undergraduate students, this index of growth in circulation tends to shrink even further. One of the marked features of American educational development in the last two decades has been the growth of graduate school enrolments. The increase in the number of graduate students for the 23 institutions in Mr. White's study is not given, and a change in the method of classification made it impossible to calculate it from the published figures. For the country as a whole however, this increase has been very evident. In the 10 years 1925-26 to 1934-35 the number of theses submitted for the doctor of philosophy degree increased 88 per cent.[4] The U. S. Office of Education figures give an increase of 109 per cent in the number of doctorates conferred in the 9 year period 1926-27 to 1935-36. The growth in the number of graduate students outran that of undergraduates to a considerable degree. Most librarians will agree that a decided increase in the per cent of graduate students in a student body will result in an increase in the total library circulation, even granting that such students usually have stack permits. How much of the annual per capita increase of 2 per cent which Mr. White's study indicates can be attributed to this factor, it is impossible to say, but its influence can scarcely be denied.

We may conclude then that there has been during recent years a considerable increase in the circulation of libraries due to enlarged enrolments, increase in the number of graduate students and other factors, the

[4]*Ibid.*, p.24. The figures are from the American Council on Education.

total process resulting in a small increase in the use of the library per individual student. For undergraduates this would appear to be something less, on the average, than two per cent per year. Whether this growth justifies the adjective "inspiring" which Mr. White feels warranted in using, opinions will differ.[5] Perhaps all will agree that the growth has not been rapid enough to warrant a complacent conclusion that the problem of undergraduate use of the library has been solved. Agreement on this point will possibly be reinforced by the figures to be cited below.

An improvement in the book circulation is important, but the more interesting question is what the present usage is. Most librarians keep figures recording the use made of their book collections, and these figures are usually published in the annual reports and gathered up into statistical tables in the *Bulletin* of the American Library Association and elsewhere. Librarians have always recognized their defects, however, as a gauge of the amount of reading done, and, consequently, for any comparative or cumulative purposes. There are two defects, in particular which render these figures unusable for the present purposes:

1. In the first place the circulation figures have different meanings in practically every library in which they are recorded. One library with closed stacks and closed reserve book collections is able to count almost every book that is used, with the exception of the reference collection. In another with open stacks, and with special reading rooms where books in constant demand are on open shelves, there is a large percentage of use which leaves no statistical result. The second library may actually report a lower circulation average while being more frequently used. Circulation figures thus must in each case be interpreted by means

[5]It is only fair to add that Mr. White was not considering the student problem primarily, but rather the accomplishments of and trends in American university libraries.

of a knowledge of what it is that is being counted. These additional data unfortunately cannot be added up in the column. In other words, in keeping circulation records the libraries do not count the same things, and the figures reported are not units of the same order.

2. The second defect of these figures for the present purpose is their inclusive character. In practically every library the count of circulation includes book withdrawals by undergraduates, graduate students, faculty members, members of the library and administrative staffs, alumni and residents of the local community, all combined into one grand circulation total. As a partial measure of the work which the library does this figure is no doubt serviceable, but as a guide to the amount of undergraduate reading it is completely misleading. Any averages obtained by dividing into this total the number of students or the number of students plus the number of faculty members are quite undependable. They bestow upon the undergraduates the credit in part for the heavier reading of faculty members and graduate students and also for all the loans to readers outside the academic group. Two illustrations will show the erroneous results which such calculations can yield. An analysis of the circulation of the Haverford College Library for 1936-37 showed that of the 26,275 loans made from the main library only 62 per cent were to students of the college. A similar analysis for the Woman's College of Rochester University for the same year indicated that only 48 per cent of the loans were to regularly enrolled students of that college.[6]

For these reasons it is plain that any accurate con-

[6]The distributions in the two cases were as follows: Haverford College: loans to faculty, 16 per cent; to students, 62 per cent; to borrowers not connected with the college, 22 per cent. Woman's College of Rochester University: students, 48 per cent; Men's College students, 5 per cent; extension students, 8 per cent; faculty and administration, 17 per cent; Eastman School of Music, 4 per cent; city borrowers, including graduates of the University, 18 per cent.

clusions as to how much undergraduates use their respective libraries will have to rest on special studies in which these variations and ambiguities are eliminated or controlled. Even such special studies are never completely accurate, but a number of these, particularly if they involve fairly large groups, will yield results which may be regarded as statistically correct and dependable. Efforts have been made to collect all the more important studies of this sort and to clarify uncertainties of terminology and procedure by correspondence with those who carried them out. Certain additional studies were completed also. How much these agree with each other will be evident from the discussion which follows.

1. One may begin with the study of the college library made by Waples and others for the North Central Association. This study was interested in getting a basis for the evaluation or comparison of different libraries. For this purpose it was believed that the reserve book circulation figures were useless. The study therefore was confined to withdrawal of books from the general collections of the libraries. It was found that renewals constituted so small a proportion of the free circulation that "they could be omitted without loss and with considerable saving of clerical labor." Thirty-five colleges were studied, the records being kept for periods varying from 70 to 110 days and equated to a common base. Waples sums up the results as follows: "The mean number of titles borrowed per student per semester for the 35 colleges is 5.55 titles, the institutional averages ranging from 1.8 to 16.35."[7]

This study of undergraduate reading in 35 colleges is the most comprehensive which has been made. Waples states that in the selection of colleges studied "the attempt was made to represent a normal range of institutional excellence and to include all the princi-

[7] Douglas Waples, *et. al., The Library* ("Evaluation of Higher Institutions," No. 4; Chicago: University of Chicago Press, 1936), p.55.

pal types of institutions with which the Association has to deal."[8] This conscious selection of a range of excellence is reflected apparently in the range of the institutional averages.

2. During the spring semester of 1932-33 Mr. E. W. McDiarmid, Jr., made a most careful study of the reading of undergraduates in seven liberal arts colleges. A total number of 2,278 students were involved, being about equally divided between men and women. Records of loans of books from the general collection and of books on reserve were kept separately. The former were separated into curricula and non-curricula groups. In the case of the reserved book collections both the total number of book withdrawals and the number of different titles involved were counted. The results of this analysis are embodied in part in the following table, the word "free" meaning from the general book collection:

TABLE 1*

MEAN NUMBER OF BOOK CHARGES AND OF TITLES LOANED, ONE SEMESTER,
TO STUDENTS IN SEVEN COLLEGES

College	Mean No. of Free Curricular Titles	Mean No. of Free Extra-curricular Titles	Mean No. of Re-served Charges	Mean No. of Re-served Titles
E	2.57	1.26	37.49	19.49
D	9.65	1.38	35.77	19.37
A	4.69	2.44	24.27	12.58
G	3.26	1.19	26.38	10.48
C	1.43	1.61	19.67	8.43
B	6.32	3.31	24.50	8.41
F	7.96	1.47	20.63	7.92
Mean for 7 colleges	5.12	1.81	26.95	12.38

*E. W. McDiarmid, Jr., "Conditions Affecting the Use of the College Library," *Library Quarterly*, V (1935), Table IX, 70.
[8]*Ibid.*, p.3.

The addition of columns one and two indicates an average use of 6.93 volumes per student from the general collections of the colleges. The agreement with Waples' figure, 5.55, for 35 colleges is striking. One notes also agreement of the two studies in the range of the institutional averages. McDiarmid's averages for the "free" loans range from 3.04 volumes per semester per student to 11.03 (columns one and two). Combining the free and the reserve book loans into a single figure (*i.e.*, adding columns one, two and four in Table 1) the range is considerably reduced. The institutional differences—using McDiarmid's own summary—are then seen to be as follows:

TABLE 2*

MEAN NUMBER OF TITLES BORROWED PER SEMESTER
BY STUDENTS OF SEVEN COLLEGES

College	Mean Equated to Represent 98 Days Each
A	19.70
B	18.04
C	11.46
D	29.40
E	23.32
F	17.35
G	14.93
Mean for the Seven Colleges	19.17

*E. W. McDiarmid, Jr., "Conditions Affecting the Use of the College Library," *Library Quarterly*, V (1935), Table V, 64.

McDiarmid compares these differences between the several colleges with the differences found between the loans to men students in the seven colleges and to women students, between the averages of the four academic classes, and between those of different scholarship groups. The institutional differences are greater than any of these.

3. A study of the use of the college library in five colleges of the Middle West has recently been com-

pleted by Mr. Harry L. Johnson.[9] The student enrolment in these colleges ranged from 238 to 675, the combined enrolment being 2,438, a slightly greater number than in McDiarmid's investigation. These also were almost equally divided between men and women. Mr. Johnson's study covered the entire academic year.

This investigation undertook to answer two questions: To what extent do students make use of their college libraries? To what extent are the books in the libraries used? At the moment I am concerned with the former question.

The students in these five colleges were studied as a single group. Mr. Johnson concluded for reasons that are eminently sound that the median rather than the mean is the better of the two indicators. In his carefully prepared tables, however, he gives the data by which the mean can be calculated. For purposes of comparison with the other studies cited, I have made this calculation.

The median student in Mr. Johnson's group of 2,438 withdrew 6.79 volumes from the general collection of his college library. For an interesting reason which will be discussed later, the median is much lower than the mean. The mean number of withdrawals per student for the year was 11.36 books, or 12.54 including renewals. This is almost exactly the average shown in the other studies. In the case of the reserve book collection, the median was 20.26 different titles per student, or 42.5 charges; the mean (calculated from the data presented), 26.19 titles per student, or 60.87 charges or withdrawals.[10] In both types

[9] "A Study of the Use of Five College Libraries" (Unpublished Master's thesis, University of Iowa, 1938). I am greatly indebted both to Mr. Johnson and to Dean Packer who directed the study for making available to me the results of this investigation previous to its publication. The study has proven so fruitful that it has been extended to include a number of other colleges. The figures quoted here must therefore be regarded as preliminary and tentative.

[10] In the case of reserve readings figures are available from only four colleges.

of reading women students withdrew appreciably
more volumes than did the men.

4. The last two studies have dealt with groups of
colleges having enrolments of less than a thousand
students and located in the Middle West. Two investigations of undergraduate use of the library in eastern institutions are now to be placed beside these.
The first of these was directed by the present writer.
The institution studied is located east of the Appa-
lachians in a small town where supplementary library
facilities are practically nonexistent, is large enough
to make the results of the inquiry statistically valuable, has an undoubtedly excellent faculty and a good
library. To preserve the anonymity necessary for objective discussion, as well as to carry out certain obligations, the institution will be referred to as University A. If this study is described in more detail than
those above, it is not because of a belief in its superior
accuracy or importance, but because the data have not
been published or made available in other ways.

The university in question had an official enrolment for the year of the study of 2,547 undergraduates, about a third of them being women students.
After eliminating those who dropped out during the
year and others for whom the records were not complete, there remained 2,292 names on the roll. The
stacks of the library were closed to undergraduates at
the time, and the reserved collections were transferred
to closed shelves for the period of the study. Except
for reference tools, periodicals, newspapers, and manuscripts, a record was thus secured of all use made of
the book collections of the general library. The survey
covered the second half of the spring semester of
1936-37, a period of nine weeks.

All such studies contain their margin of error. Two
omissions in this study should be mentioned. There
are three professional school libraries on the campus.
They are technical and professional in contents and

atmosphere, and except for those seniors admitted to the Schools, undergraduates make almost no use of them. The names of such seniors were withdrawn from the study, but no allowance was made for the occasional use of those collections by other undergraduates. Several scientific departmental libraries offered a different problem. Difficulties in securing accurate records of their use resulted in a decision to eliminate these departmental libraries from the study but to allow for the reading done in the following manner: Class enrolment in those departments was fractionally more than 10 per cent of the total undergraduate registration. On the assumption that the use of the library by these departments of science—all of them using laboratory methods of instruction—was equal in proportion to the use by other departments, the results recorded below should be increased by 10 per cent. Since it is generally believed that classes in the laboratory sciences use the library less than other departments on the whole, this 10 per cent addition would certainly seem to cover or exceed the facts in the case.[11] One further question concerning the value of the figures had to be answered. The study embraced the second half of the semester. Did library reading fall off with the approach of spring? In this institution, in the year studied, it did not. Records of both the reserve book room and of the general circulation showed that more than 50 per cent of the total reading fell in the second half of the semester. Final examinations and collegiate procrastination were apparently more important influences than the spring sunshine.

A summary of the average use of the library made by the undergraduates of the institution appears in the following tables. Table 3 gives figures for loans

[11]The general impression that the natural sciences use the library less than other departments is statistically proved in the case of the seven colleges studied by McDiarmid. See E. W. McDiarmid, Jr., "Conditions Affecting the Use of the College Library," *Library Quarterly*, V (1935), Table VI, 66.

from the general collection. Renewals, in line with the experience of Waples and others, were not counted.

TABLE 3
GENERAL CIRCULATION BOOK WITHDRAWALS, NINE WEEKS,
UNIVERSITY A

Class	No. of Students	Total No. of With-drawals	Average No. of Withdrawals per Student
Senior	415	2,059	4.97
Junior	526	1,805	3.43
Sophomore	659	1,577	2.24
Freshmen	692	1,143	1.79
All	2,292	6,584	2.87
Adding ten per cent for use of science libraries			3.16

In the case of reserve books renewals were counted in making up the figures.[12]

TABLE 4
RESERVE BOOK WITHDRAWALS, NINE WEEKS,
UNIVERSITY A

Class	No. of Students	Total No. of With-drawals	Average No. of Withdrawals per Student
Senior	415	5,798	14
Junior	526	8,758	16
Sophomore	659	7,433	11
Freshmen	692	4,997	7
All	2,292	26,986	11.76
Adding ten per cent for use of science libraries			12.94

[12]When this study was initiated the primary question in mind was, How much do the students use the library? In the case of books on reserve, the use of which was limited to so short a period as to permit the reading of only a portion of the book, it seemed necessary to know how many times these books were borrowed. Unfortunately, the study was well under way before the writer realized the value of knowing also how many titles were involved in this number of withdrawals. The full picture is only secured by keeping both figures, as in McDiarmid's study.

5. College B is an excellent eastern liberal arts college for men with a better than average library. A study of the extent of student use of the general collection for a period of nine weeks was made in the spring of 1937, and repeated in the fall semester of 1938-39. For the latter period 836 students withdrew 4,349 volumes, an average of 5.2 per student. The reserve reading was not studied during the period.

6. In the fall of 1930 Professor A. C. Eurich studied the use of the library of the University of Minnesota.[13] The number of call slips to be tabulated, had the study lasted a full quarter, would have been so enormous that it was found necessary to base the study on what was believed to be a typical week. While this admittedly was not final, it was felt that it would be indicative. The latter half of the tenth week of the fall quarter and the first of the eleventh week were chosen for this purpose.

The study was confined to the records of the general library only. A number of divisions of the University have branch libraries. To meet this difficulty, "the number of students in each division of the University with a separate branch library was deducted from the total in order to arrive at a figure that would be somewhat representative of the student body which might be expected to use the general library." The total number of students in the fall quarter, extension division excluded, was 12,153; deducting those in the colleges of medicine, engineering, chemistry, mines, agriculture and law, there remained 8,362. The total circulation for the typical week was 2,749 volumes from the general collection and 8,011 charges at the reserve book desk. Professor Eurich formulated his conclusions in terms of the ratio of the average daily withdrawals to the number of the student body using this library, the figure being 5.6 per cent for the general collection and 15.9 per cent for the reserve books. By

[13]"Student Use of the Library," *Library Quarterly*, III (1933), 87-94.

multiplying his figures for the typical week by 36, however, an annual averaged circulation can be calculated which can be compared with the others cited in this chapter. This calculation indicates an average circulation of 11.8 volumes per student per year from the general collection and 34.4 volumes per student from the books placed on reserve. The former of these is quite in line with the averages cited from other institutions, the latter somewhat lower. Professor Eurich concludes that "the proportion of students who use the library each day is a relatively small part of the entire student body."

This study is interesting as giving an indication of the amount of reading in a large state university.

7. In the fall of 1934 Dr. Ralph H. Parker, now of Pomona College, studied the general circulation of the University of Texas library.[14] The period covered was from October 15th to December 15th, a total of 62 days, or shortly less than nine weeks. During the observation period there was a total circulation of 19,492 loans, of which 11,330 issues were to undergraduate students in the College of Liberal Arts. The registrar's office has informed me that in the fall term of that year there were 4,394 students enrolled in this college. This yields an average per student circulation for the period of 2.57 withdrawals per student. Equated to an annual basis this would give slightly more than 10.28 volumes per student.

These several studies may now be summarized and compared. All of them are based on first hand examination of the withdrawal slips of undergraduate students. It will be noted that 51 institutions are involved and over 20,000 students, in addition to the enrolments in the 35 colleges whose records were summarized by Waples. The agreement of these studies is very striking. Though questions might be raised as to

[14]Dr. Parker kindly made available to me his unpublished manuscript describing this study.

TABLE 5

SUMMARY OF GENERAL CIRCULATION AVERAGES, FIFTY-FIVE INSTITUTIONS

Study	Group Studied	Period	Av. per Student	Student Av. Equated to Academic Year
1 Waples	35 colleges	one semester	5.55	11.10
2 McDiarmid	2,278 students in 7 colleges	one semester	6.93	13.86
3 Johnson	2,438 students in 5 colleges	one year	11.36	11.36
4 Univ. A	2,292 students in 1 univ.	one half semester	3.16	12.64
5 College B	836 students in 1 college	one semester	5.20	10.40
6 Eurich	8,362 students in 1 univ.	typical week	0.33	11.80
7 Parker	4,394 students in 1 univ.	one half semester	2.57	10.28

the accuracy of the method employed in one or two of the studies, their results strongly confirm one another.

Figures of use of the reserve book collections admittedly rest on a narrower base, but Table 6 on the following page summarizes the reading of 6,333 undergraduates in 12 colleges.

These tables include, I believe, all of the important circulation studies which have been published in recent years, as well as some others which have not been published. In addition to the studies listed here, several others have been secured which come from institutions of a special type, most of them small. These latter call for special treatment and discussion, and

TABLE 6

SUMMARY RESERVE BOOK CIRCULATION AVERAGES, TWELVE INSTITUTIONS

Study	Group Studied	Period	Av. No. of Titles per Student	Av. No. of Charges per Student	Av. Equated to One Year	
					Titles	Charges
2 (McDiarmid)	2,278 students in 7 colleges	one semester	12.38	26.95	24.76	53.90
3 (Johnson)	1,763 students in 4 colleges	one year	26.19	60.87	26.19	60.87
4 (Univ. A)	2,292 univ. students in 1	one half semester	. . . . .	12.94	. . . . .	51.76

this is postponed for the moment. The above figures seem to warrant one in drawing the conclusion that if one will examine the library records of a sufficiently large number of college students taught in the usual manner, he will find that the average student draws from the general collection of his college or university library about 12 books per year. This, it requires no advanced mathematics to discover, is 6 per semester, or slightly more than one book per course. In addition to the use of the general collection to this extent, this undergraduate, on the average, seems to make from 50 to 60 withdrawals per year from the reserve book collection, approximately half that many titles being involved. Using the higher figure, this would mean reading portions of about 15 titles per semester or three per course.

Several objections to or qualifications of these statements must be considered immediately. The first is that there are many institutions in which this average is very considerably exceeded. This, happily, is true.

We shall return to the point later; at the moment one need only remark that it appears to be equally true that there are others which fall below this general average.[15]

A second objection is that the above figures do not include a number of the important functions of the college library. In addition to the use of books in the stacks and on reserve, one must add that of the encyclopedias and other reference tools, maps, newspapers and periodicals. Protests have been made against the use of book circulation figures, as a measurement of library usefulness. In 1934 Gaskill, Dunbar and Brown made a count of students entering the library building of Iowa State College for certain typical days. Using this data they estimated, in opposition to Eurich's conclusions, that 47 per cent used the library daily. Inquiry was made in short interviews at the exit as to the purpose for which the students had come. According to the answers given, 14 per cent came to use the newspapers; 9 per cent for general reading (books and magazines); 51 per cent for assigned reading; 25 per cent for problems or topics; 8 per cent for specific books other than assigned reading; 7 per cent to use their own books; and 9 per cent gave reasons other than reading.[16] There can be no doubt

[15]In the case of two well-known statements of circulation averages a word of explanation is in order. In Douglas Waples, *et. al., op. cit.,* p.57, the average home circulation of 233 colleges and universities is given as 19 per student per year. In W. M. Randall and F. L. Goodrich, *Principles of College Library Administration* (Chicago: A.L.A. and University of Chicago Press, 1936), p.213 an average for 95 colleges for the year 1933-34 is given as 28.4, and for 20 colleges "giving better than average service" as 33.8. In both cases, Mr. Randall informs me, the figures were reached by dividing the recorded home or general circulation by the number of students. This credited students with the reading of faculty, local residents and other groups. In the light of this information the average of 19 for the 233 institutions seems confirmatory of the figure of approximately 12 reached above rather than the opposite. Mr. Randall while suggesting that perhaps the higher averages for the 95 colleges may have been due to a better selection, is inclined to minimize the value of all such circulation figures. (Correspondence May 21 and 24, 1938.)

[16]H. V. Gaskill, R. M. Dunbar and C. H. Brown, "An Analytical Study of the Use of a College Library," *Library Quarterly,* IV (October, 1934), 564-87.

that many undergraduates use the library for purposes other than to draw out books. The value of these other services is not denied, but it is contended that these other activities are built around and related to the use of the book collection and that indications of the extent of this use will reveal perhaps better than any other single approach the significance of the library's contribution to the education of college students.

A third objection to the averages stated above calls for more detailed discussion. Granting the correctness of the figures, their value may be questioned. There is no such thing as the "average student," or more correctly, there are only a limited number of them. A single arithmetical mean is not a sufficient description of the library borrowings of so many thousands of students. Can these figures be broken up in any more instructive fashion?

This question can be answered in the affirmative. In a sufficient number of these studies to make the results significant, an important additional fact can be demonstrated.

I begin with the study of University A. In the case of these 2,292 students it will be recalled that the average number of borrowings from the general collection was 2.87 per student for the nine weeks of that observation period. In an effort to determine the cause of this low average, a count was made of the number of students who made a negligible use of the library. This was defined as the withdrawal of less than one book per month. When these figures were grouped according to the four academic classes, the astonishing table which appears on the next page (Table 7) resulted.

It will be noted that 42 per cent of the students made no use at all of the general collection during the period studied. More than two thirds of the undergraduate student body, 66.9 per cent, made a negligible use of it according to the definition employed.

TABLE 7

STUDENTS MAKING NEGLIGIBLE USE OF GENERAL BOOK COLLECTION
UNIVERSITY A—SECOND HALF OF SPRING SEMESTER

Class	No. of Students	Total No. of Withdrawals	Av. No. of Withdrawals per Student	Number of Students Withdrawing:				Per Cent of Students Using 0, 1, or 2 Vols.
				0 Vols.	1 Vol.	2 Vols.	0, 1 or 2 Vols.	
Senior	415	2,059	4.97	119	49	45	213	51.0
Junior	526	1,805	3.43	175	75	63	313	59.0
Sophomore	659	1,577	2.24	296	115	67	478	72.0
Freshman	692	1,143	1.79	369	93	68	530	76.0
All	2,292	6,584	2.87	959	332	243	1,534	66.9

The facts can be stated a third way. By adding columns four and five above one learns that 1,291 students or 53.8 per cent of the undergraduate student body withdrew 332 books from the central book collection. The remaining 46.2 per cent borrowed 6,252 books or 95 per cent of the total number withdrawn. Nor can this large per cent who failed to make more than a negligible use of the library be blamed solely on freshmen and sophomores, and their dependence upon textbooks. Over half of the senior class are in the same category.[17]

[17]It must be remembered that in this particular study 10 per cent of the total registration was in departments of science which made use of science libraries, the use of which was not recorded. Were these data available, the above figures, of course, would be reduced. A purely mathematical calculation, based on the assumption that the ratio of users and nonusers in the science libraries was the same as in the general library, does not reduce the above figures sufficiently to modify their significance.

A similar distribution of the reserve book withdrawals is shown in the following table:

TABLE 8

STUDENTS MAKING NEGLIGIBLE USE OF RESERVE BOOK COLLECTION
UNIVERSITY A—SECOND HALF OF SPRING SEMESTER

Class	No. of Students	Total No. of Withdrawals	Av. No. of Withdrawals per Student	Number of Students Withdrawing:				Per Cent of Students Using 0, 1 or 2 Vols.
				0 Vols.	*1 Vol.*	*2 Vols.*	*0, 1 or 2 Vols.*	
Senior	415	5,798	14	61	28	18	107	25.7
Junior	526	8,758	16	54	21	20	95	18.0
Sophomore	659	7,433	11	131	34	33	198	30.0
Freshman	692	4,997	7	189	46	42	277	40.0
All	2,292	26,986	11.76	435	129	113	677	29.5

The same general tendency is to be seen at work here, though to a less degree. The per cent of undergraduates making no use of the reserve collection during the half semester leading up to the examinations was 19; approximately 30 per cent made a negligible use of it.

Although it is advisable to tabulate separately the figures concerning the nonuse of the general collection and of the books placed on reserve, it will be of interest also to disregard these two different types of usage and to consider the use of the library as a single unit. The following table ignores any distinction between reserves and the general collection. Thus a student who withdrew during the nine weeks one book from the general collection and one volume from the reserve collection would be listed under the heading of two withdrawals.

TABLE 9

STUDENTS MAKING NEGLIGIBLE USE OF TOTAL BOOK COLLECTION
UNIVERSITY A—SECOND HALF OF SPRING SEMESTER

Class	No. of Students	Total No. of Book Withdrawals	Withdrawals per Student	Number of Students Using:			
				0 Vols.	1 Vol.	2 Vols.	0, 1 or 2 Vols.
Senior	415	7,857	19	32	21	13	66
Junior	526	10,563	20	30	13	20	63
Sophomore	659	9,010	14	91	41	25	157
Freshman	692	6,140	11	140	44	41	225
All	2,292	33,570	14.64	293*	119	99	511†

*Thus 12.7 per cent of the students involved used no library books.
†This means that 22.29 per cent of the students involved used not more than 2 library books.

Mr. Johnson gives the distribution of loans among the undergraduates of the colleges which he studied. Since his figures are for the entire academic year, the negligible use, arbitrarily defined as less than one book per month, is eight for the year. From his figures for general reading Table 10 has been prepared.

On the basis of the entire year, the per cent making no use of the library in these 5 colleges was 10.6. Those withdrawing fewer than one volume per month totaled 55 per cent of the combined student bodies. One notes again that it is not freshmen and sophomores only who are responsible for these figures.

The distribution of the reserve book reading in these lower brackets for the four colleges included in this part of Johnson's investigation is shown in Table 11:

TABLE 10

STUDENTS MAKING NEGLIGIBLE USE OF GENERAL COLLECTION
FIVE COLLEGES—NINE MONTHS

Class	No. of Students	No. Using 0 Vols.	No. Using 1-4 Vols.	No. Using 5-8 Vols.	Total Using 0-8 Vols.	Per Cent Withdrawing 0-8 Vols.
Senior	394	25	68	62	155	39.30
Junior	470	37	100	77	214	45.57
Sophomore	602	63	156	117	336	55.80
Freshman	972	134	281	238	653	67.00
All	2,438	259	605	494	1,358	55.00

TABLE 11

STUDENTS MAKING NEGLIGIBLE USE OF RESERVE BOOK COLLECTION
FOUR COLLEGES—NINE MONTHS

Class	No. of Students	No. Withdrawing 0 Vols.	No. Withdrawing 1-4 Vols.	No. Withdrawing 5-8 Vols.	No. Withdrawing 0-8 Vols.	Per Cent of Class Withdrawing 0-8 Vols.
Senior	274	2	6	11	19	6.9
Junior	319	1	13	24	38	11.9
Sophomore	442	18	30	34	82	18.3
Freshman	728	48	117	88	253	34.7
All	1,763	69	166	157	392	22.2

33

McDiarmid does not publish in his study the distribution by individuals or by classes. His summary, however, includes the following statement: "Still more noteworthy is the fact that twenty per cent of the students borrowed in all [general and reserves combined] five titles or less."[18] Since McDiarmid's study was for one semester, his measure of five books for the period of four and a half months is roughly in agreement with the one used above for negligible use of the library. The figure 20 per cent is to be compared with that of 22.29 per cent for the combined collections of University A (Table 9).

Only general reading was considered in the one semester study at College B, referred to below. Figures are available only for the number of students of the several classes who withdrew no books from the general collection. These were as follows:

TABLE 12

STUDENTS MAKING NO USE OF GENERAL COLLECTION
COLLEGE B—ONE SEMESTER

Class	No. in Class	No. Making No Use of Collection	Per Cent Making No Use of Collection
Senior	148	25	17
Junior	195	57	29
Sophomore	211	82	38
Freshman	282	142	69
All	836	306	36.6

Miss Withington of the Woman's College Library of Rochester University has figures for the number of students who made no use of the books from the gen-

[18]E. W. McDiarmid, Jr., *op. cit.,* 75.

34

eral collection during the fall semester 1937-38. There were 136 who fell in this category or 28 per cent of the student body. It is possible, however, that some of these students made use of the general library of the University four miles away. This figure is of special interest, since the average per student circulation of this library is high.

To aid the reader in comparing and evaluating these several analyses, the summaries in Table 13 and Table 14 are submitted:

TABLE 13

SUMMARY OF STUDIES OF NEGLIGIBLE USE OF GENERAL
COLLECTION, 8 INSTITUTIONS, 6,052 STUDENTS

Group of Students	Period	Per Cent Withdrawing 0 Books	Per Cent Withdrawing Less than One Book Per Month
2,292 students in one university	one half semester	42.0	66.9
2,438 students in five colleges	one year	10.6	55.0
836 men students in one college	one semester	36.6	....
486 women students in one college	one semester	28.0	....

The variation in the percentages withdrawing no books whatever is related of course to the duration of the period of investigation. Nor is the figure perhaps of great importance, since the withdrawal of a single book—whether it be *How to Play Tennis* or a book of fiction—removed one from this class. The comparable and more significant figures are to be found in the right hand columns of the two tables.

35

TABLE 14

SUMMARY OF STUDIES OF NEGLIGIBLE USE OF RESERVE BOOK
COLLECTION, 12 INSTITUTIONS, 6,333 STUDENTS

Group of Students	Period	Per Cent Withdrawing 0 Books	Per Cent Withdrawing Less than One Book Per Month
2,292 students in one university	one half semester	19.0	29.5
1,763 students in four colleges	one year	3.9	22.2
2,278 students in seven colleges	one semester	. . . .	20.0 ("borrowed in all 5 titles or less")

In the light of these figures one can summarize more exactly the facts which underlie the figures of average use presented in the first part of this chapter. The average number of books borrowed per year from the general collections seems to be about twelve per student, but the average would be lower were it not for the presence of a small number of students who take out a great many books. The mass of the undergraduates make very little use of the main book collection. The medians are lower than the average in each case, where both figures are known. Thus in Johnson's study where the average is 12.54 per student, for the year, the median is 6.79 books. In the University A study the average for the nine weeks of 2.87 books must be compared with a median of 1.56. Putting this in annual terms the median would be 6.24 books where the average is 11.48. In College B the average and median for the nine weeks of the first study were respectively 3 and 1.34.

In the case of the reserve books the situation is not

so clear. This may be because the measure of negligible use chosen—less than one book from reserves per month—was for this class of material too low. Nevertheless, one finds from a fifth to nearly a third of the students making virtually no use of the reserve collection. The medians again are lower than the averages. In only two of the above studies are the medians or the means of calculating them given. In the Johnson study where the average number of reserve titles borrowed is 26.19 and of reserve charges 60.87 per student, the correlative medians are 20.26 titles and 42.5 charges per student for the year. In the University A study the average number of reserve book charges for the nine weeks was 11.76 but the median was 6.92 charges.

From the data in this chapter it seems clear enough that undergraduates do not make very much use of the college or university book collection, not nearly so much as is ordinarily assumed. The fact is obscured first by total circulation figures which in practically every institution include the borrowings of everybody in the neighborhood, and by the presence in each institution of a small percentage of students who borrow a large number of books, some of them an amazing number. Since undergraduate use of the library is predominantly for curricula purposes, the above statement can be restated as follows: it seems evident that college faculties are making only a very limited use of the library in their teaching work. In a number of colleges there seem to be better libraries than are needed. This seems to demonstrate what was asserted in the previous chapter, that in spite of all its growth the library has not been fully integrated into the major program of the college. This is as true from the faculty side as from that of the library itself.

This leads to a final point. Always it must be emphasized that the averages and medians given above are for large numbers of students. It is not claimed that these figures will be found to be true on every campus. The contrary is indicated. In the above studies where groups of colleges have been involved, one of the most marked features has been the variation between institutions. In McDiarmid's study, for example, the institutional differences showed a greater range than those of sex, academic class, or scholarship rating. Those colleges which have much heavier circulations merely prove the fact that the library can be made to play a larger part in the program of instruction than it seems to be doing in the majority of cases.

CHAPTER THREE

Scholarship Standing
and Library Usage

THE INVESTIGATIONS REVIEWED IN THE PREVIOUS CHAP-
ter revealed the existence of a large percentage of undergraduates who make such a slight use of the college
library that they would scarcely miss it if it ceased to
exist. The facts so startlingly portrayed by the figures
suggest that the subject be pursued one step further.
Who are the undergraduates who do not use the library? Are they the misfits and failures, along with
others who barely get by, but who are retained by college authorities in the hope of some later blossoming
of talents heretofore unrevealed? Does this large percentage of students who are indifferent to the resources of knowledge offered by the library indicate
that students to that extent have been accepted for
college enrolment who cannot use the opportunities
which it offers, or is the explanation rather that under
present methods of instruction these students do not
find a use of the library necessary or essential? In other
words, where lies the difficulty, with the student, the
instructor or the library?

There have been practically no studies of this specific problem. Several aspects of the general relation
of library usage and scholastic accomplishment have
been investigated. Thus it is indicated by a number
of detailed studies that women students in coeducational institutions use the library more consistently
than do men students. A comparison of the grades of
these same two groups in one of the studies shows a

slightly higher average for the women.[1] It is also established that the average book withdrawals of the four academic classes generally increase as one proceeds from the freshman to the senior status.[2] The facts responsible in this case are several: a process of selection by the elimination of the poorer students, greater emphasis upon individual study in the upper classes, fuller acquaintance with the library and its contents, and the general effect of the educational process. The average grade received also tends to increase with the progress up the academic ladder, probably for the same reasons.

McDiarmid in his study of seven colleges included among the subjects investigated the relation of the number of books borrowed by each student to his scholastic attainment. Only a very slight correlation was observable. The coefficient for the entire group of 2,278 students was $+ .173 \pm 0.20$. He concluded that "the number of titles read by each student has little to do with the grade point average."[3]

A different result was obtained, however, when the students' records were divided into four groups according to the grade which was received and the correlation examined for the groups as units. The facts then appeared as in Table 15 (page 41) which I have simplified somewhat from McDiarmid's presentation.

This contradiction in result depending upon the way the data are handled is not elucidated by McDiarmid, but the following explanation seems to be the most likely: a lack of correlation between books borrowed and grades received may be due to either of

[1] E. W. McDiarmid, Jr.,"Conditions Affecting the Use of the College Library," *Library Quarterly*, V (1935) , 61. The grade point average for men in the 7 colleges investigated was 2.88, for women 3.06. The average number of books withdrawn by the men was 13.17 as compared with 22.17 by the women.

[2] Not universally, however. In one careful record the juniors withdrew in the year of the investigation slightly more books than the seniors. Teaching methods affect the figures also.

[3] McDiarmid, *op. cit.*, p. 63.

Scholarship Standing and Library Usage

TABLE 15*

MEAN NUMBER OF TITLES BORROWED BY STUDENTS
GROUPED ACCORDING TO SCHOLARSHIP

Scholarship Group	No. in Group	Mean No. of Titles Borrowed
3.60 — 5.00 (B average or above)	557	22.65
2.60 — 3.59 (C average to B)	1,123	19.10
1.60 — 2.59 (D average to C)	644	16.61
0.20 — 1.59 (Lower than D average)	64	11.56

*E. W. McDiarmid, Jr., "Conditions Affecting the Use of the College Library," *Library Quarterly*, V (1935), Table IV, 63.

two types of divergence, good grades with little reading or bad grades with much reading. Both relationships appear in any considerable set of records, but the latter seems to be proportionately less frequent. There is some positive evidence that students who read widely generally do better than average, though the relationship may not necessarily be causative. The students who do read widely are responsible, we have seen, for a large part of the total borrowing from the library.[4] Their book withdrawals distributed for the most part in the upper two of McDiarmid's scholarship brackets would bring these group averages to their higher level of library borrowings in spite of the presence in the same brackets of other students who had evidenced little interest in the library or its contents.

[4]For example, in University A it was noted that 46 per cent of the students were responsible for 95 per cent of the general circulation. The calculation can be narrowed still further from the data supplied in Table 7: 33.1 per cent of the students were responsible for 87.6 per cent of the general circulation.

In other words, the higher average borrowing of the upper scholastic groups seems likely to be due to a portion of the students in these groups, whose high borrowing records were sufficient to raise the average of the group, while the lack of correlation when the records were worked individually is accounted for by the existence also of many students with good grades who did little reading. Corroboration of the existence of this condition and its validity as an explanation of the divergence encountered above is to be found in the further details of this chapter.

Corroboration of McDiarmid's inability to find a consistent correlation between library usage and grades given students, except by treating them in large groups, is supplied by two other studies. Professor A. C. Eurich, whose study of undergraduate reading in a large university has already been mentioned, made a second and more detailed investigation of the reading of 347 undergraduates in the University of Minnesota.[5] The group was divided first into those who used the university library and those who did not. A statistically significant difference in scholarship rating was observed between the two groups. This difference amounted to "almost one half the distance from a letter grade of C to a letter grade of B." Since for this part of the study no freshmen were included, this difference while statistically "significant," would not seem to be very great. No relationship could be detected, however, when the attention was directed to the amount of reading done by individual students and their scholarship rating. The coefficient of correlation here was .02. Eurich refused to draw the conclusion that the use of the library was responsible for the slightly higher grades received by the library users over the non-users. "The higher scholarship and a desire to use the library may both be due to a third

[5]"The Significance of Library Reading among College Students," *School and Society*, XXXVI (1932), 92ff.

factor such as drive or motivation which is altogether too elusive to isolate at the present stage of progress."[6]

The second study bearing out this conclusion was made recently in a small college in Pennsylvania which, by agreement, will be referred to as College C. In February 1936 the dean requested of the librarian a summary of the facts concerning the use of the library by students and faculty members. The library secured the data, most of it quite in line with the figures presented in the previous chapter, but went further and investigated the correlation between grades received by the individual members of the graduating classes of 1934, 1935, 1936 and 1937 and the extent of their library use. The coefficient of correlation of 18 seniors of the class of 1934 and the number of books borrowed was —.03; of the 21 members of the class of 1935 +.27; of the 18 seniors of 1936 —.05; and of the 26 graduates of 1937 +.44.

This lack of correlation between grades of individual students and their borrowings from the library may not prove very much. Too many different factors are at work. In the first place, in so many cases the grades used include those of courses in which library materials play little part in the plan of instruction. Laboratory sciences and courses in mathematics are obviously of this character. Students taking a major part of their work in these departments would naturally make little use of the library, though their academic work might be above criticism. Every such case would lower the ratio of correlation. Other factors tending to invalidate any conclusions drawn from a general lack of correlation might be the purchase of reading material by some students, the use of other libraries, the fact that books borrowed may deal with subjects other than those studied in courses, plus the possibility that some at least of the books borrowed may not be read, or if read, not understood. In view

[6]*Ibid.*, p.96.

of these various factors it would seem to be useless to attempt to press any conclusion drawn from such lack of correlation. If, however, these factors could be controlled, or very considerably reduced in their influence, valid and highly interesting conclusions might be reached.

In the study of the undergraduate reading of University A this opportunity seemed to offer itself. There are no other libraries accessible to the students of this institution except a small public library whose collection consists primarily of fiction. There is no bookstore in the town carrying a stock of books other than a few popular titles of the month. The bookstore on the campus sells little other than specified class textbooks. In this situation the complicating factors seemed to be reduced to a minimum.

To eliminate other factors, such as the withdrawal of books having nothing to do with the courses of instruction or the failure to use those withdrawn, the usual approach to this problem was reversed. Instead of studying the scholastic records of those who took out varying numbers of books, attention was directed to those students who did not withdraw books from the library. Such students in the situation described were evidently doing their work without the use of library resources.[7] By referring to Table 9 it will be seen that 12.7 per cent of this student body withdrew no books from the library during the period studied and that 22.29 per cent borrowed less than one per month. The latter group was chosen for examination, since it gave a larger number to be studied. These 511 students were divided among the four academic classes. How did they fare scholastically?

[7]Two exceptions to this statement are recognized: a few individuals may have purchased the books needed in all of their courses, and some others may have used books borrowed for them by their friends. The latter no doubt happens frequently, but that a sufficient number of students depended upon their friends continuously for nine weeks, within which fell the period of preparation for the final examinations, to affect significantly the results is considered unlikely.

As remarked above, there are a number of courses in which the answer to this question would have little significance, namely, in the case of those in which little use of the library is usually expected. All courses in the natural sciences therefore were eliminated from consideration, as well as those in mathematics, engineering and physical education. Certain other courses, though of questionable value for the purpose, were not eliminated. Foreign language courses were retained, since the most approved methods of instruction in this field call for rapid reading of the language and also the use of descriptive materials on the country and culture studied. Though particular courses in other fields might justifiably make no use of the library, no attempt was made to remove them from the study, largely because of difficulties of definition, but also in part because the object of this phase of the investigation was to determine to what extent students apparently do successful work without borrowing books from the library in those fields in which libraries are thought to be essential.

The facts for these students for whom grades could be supplied by the registrar's office are presented in Table 16 on page 46.

It will be observed that these students who made virtually no use of the library, on the whole, did excellently, at least in the part of their work falling in the departments of social science and of the humanities. They received more As than Fs and more Bs than Ds. Their average is better than C. In other words, according to the judgment of their instructors they did better than average work. This calls for one qualification. The average grade of all undergraduates for the semester in question was slightly better than C.[8] The average grades of the nonusers of the library

[8]The average number of quality-points per hour for all undergraduate men of this institution was 1.19; the average number of quality-points per hour for the undergraduates who made virtually no use of the library was 1.02.

TABLE 16

ANALYSIS OF GRADES OF 446 UNDERGRADUATES OF UNIVERSITY A
WHO WITHDREW NO MORE THAN 2 VOLUMES FROM ANY PART
OF THE LIBRARY—SECOND HALF OF SPRING SEMESTER

Class	Grades				
	A	B	C	D	F
Senior					
55 Men	15	60	62	19	2
6 Women	4	11	8	1	0
Junior					
40 Men	7	31	47	19	10
9 Women	3	15	9	3	0
Sophomore					
103 Men	17	65	124	66	22
23 Women	7	27	40	15	2
Freshman					
190 Men	45	139	302	118	33
20 Women	2	25	36	12	4
Total					
446 Students	100	373	628	253	73

thus was almost identical with that of the student body as a whole. Nor can this be attributed to a large number of freshmen who would be more likely to be taught by textbook methods. Excluding the freshmen, the total grades of the 236 sophomores, juniors, and seniors who made a negligible use of the library, science and mathematics course grades being excluded, were as follows: A, 53; B, 209; C, 290; D, 123; F, 36.

One must be careful not to draw from these figures the wrong conclusions. There are no grounds for asserting that these students did not deserve the better than average grades. The figures tend to prove one thing only, that in this institution it was not necessary to use the library to do better than average work in the courses involved. One can state this in several other ways. From the student's standpoint one could say these students neglected the library's resources because they found they did not need to use them in order to do acceptable work. Various explanations of the data presented may be advanced, and no doubt a number of factors are involved. Among these certainly would be dependence in a number of cases upon textbooks and class lectures, ineffective methods of examination, and failure to coordinate properly the class work and the library reading. Which of these explanations, as well as others which might be suggested, are the more important does not really matter. The fact remains that, according to the judgment of the faculty members themselves, those students of the 2,292 studied who made the least use of the library and in fact almost a complete disuse of it, did better than acceptable work in their courses. The use of the library then was not a necessary part of the instructional program, or stating the case slightly differently, the teaching program in the humanities and social sciences, taking it as a whole, does not seem to have been in serious need of a library. It is probably necessary to add that instruction in this institution has developed no peculiar or eccentric form, but is the usual program of most American colleges.

Before leaving this topic it may be of interest to note the grades received by those students who did the greatest amount of reading in the same university. The table on page 48 shows these data for all students who withdrew either 20 or more volumes during the 9 weeks from the main collection or 50 or more from the reserve book shelves.

One notes that these grades are almost uniformly good. For reasons stated it is precarious to use these figures as proof of any important conclusion, but so far as they have validity, they tend to show that the lack of correlation between library usage and scho-

TABLE 17

GRADES OF STUDENTS MAKING THE GREATEST USE OF THE LIBRARY
OF UNIVERSITY A—SECOND HALF OF SPRING SEMESTER

Class	Grades				
	A	*B*	*C*	*D*	*F*
Senior					
Men	15	19	10	4	0
Women	5	16	9	2	2
Junior					
Men	15	20	14	3	1
Women	1	16	13	2	0
Sophomore					
Men	3	12	13	2	1
Women	0	0	0	0	0
Total	39	83	59	13	4

lastic achievement is due more to nonreaders who receive high grades than to the low grades of those who
read widely.

Two further investigations of student reading in
this university illustrate and define the apparent wide
lack of integration between classroom work and library reading. One of these was to examine the reading of the reserve books set up for particular courses.
The object of this was to determine whether in a
number of typical courses the class found it necessary
to read the materials specified by the instructor as
vital to the course. In this part of the study no attention was given to books taken out from the general
stacks, since individual courses were being studied
and one could not know without the most elaborate
investigations the courses for which these books were
borrowed. It may be that students in some of the
courses referred to below secured from the general
stacks materials which met their course needs. If so,

the fact is inconsequential, since the purpose was not to express a judgment as to the validity of the grade given by the instructor, but merely how effectively the course in question was planned and conducted from the standpoint of the use of library resources.

The following tables, with some comments, show typical results of this inquiry. In general, they bear out the proposition that only slight correlation is to be observed between scholastic standing and library use, a proposition, however, which has a special pertinency when one has under consideration the particular volumes chosen by the instructor for the course. Logical objections can be made to the use of these data on the grounds that the class groups are too small to have statistical value. Individual cases—such as those of students who had done the reading in some previous experiences, or who purchased many volumes for themselves, or who withdrew books but did not read them—can produce a distorted picture. This is admitted, and the following instances are not regarded as a demonstration of the conclusion which has been advanced, but only as further illustrations of it. Since these cases are only illustrative and confirmatory, there is no reason for reproducing a great number of them. I am not sure that these presentations should be described as typical, for each class examined followed a different pattern. They will perhaps make graphic, however, the lack of consistency between reading and scholastic recognition which is constantly to be observed.

In examining the following tables it should be remembered that the figures for books borrowed cover the second half of the spring semester, including the examination period for 1937, and that these borrowings are for a maximum of three hours or over night only. The students in each class are grouped in whatever appeared to be the most natural divisions of the recorded use.

49

TABLE 18

READING OF THE CLASS RESERVE AND GRADES RECEIVED BY A
CLASS OF 27 STUDENTS STUDYING POLITICAL SCIENCE

No. of Charges	No. of Students Receiving Grades of:				
	A	B	C	D	F
10 — 16	0	2	3	0	0
5 — 9	1	2	2	1	0
2 — 4	0	0	7	0	1
0 — 1	0	1	7	0	0

In the case of this class the better grades reflect, with one exception, more reading. One notes, however, the large cluster of satisfactory grades in the 0-1 column of charges.

TABLE 19

READING OF THE CLASS RESERVE AND GRADES RECEIVED BY A
CLASS OF 25 STUDENTS STUDYING EUROPEAN HISTORY

No. of Charges	No. of Students Receiving Grades of:				
	A	B	C	D	F
10	0	0	0	0	1
5 — 7	0	0	4	0	0
3 — 4	0	4	1	2	2
1 — 2	0	2	2	0	0
0	2	1	2	0	2

This is a textbook course. The instructor, however, is said to be especially concerned with trying to interest students in wider reading. This table illustrates the way in which the present examination system seems in some cases to militate against, rather than for, such reading. In this class individual attention to the text-book seems to have been a wiser course for the student seeking higher ranking in the course. Other sections of this same course were studied and several bear out this suggestion.

TABLE 20

READING OF THE CLASS RESERVE AND GRADES RECEIVED BY A
CLASS OF 23 STUDENTS STUDYING ECONOMICS

No. of Charges	No. of Students Receiving Grades of:				
	A	B	C	D	F
7 — 11	0	1	3	1	0
4 — 6	0	1	3	1	1
2 — 3	0	2	4	0	0
0 — 1	0	0	1	4	1

In this course one notes that while the 0-1 users received quite low grades, those credited with 2-3 charges did on the whole slightly better than either of the two groups with more reading to their credit.

A third approach to the problem of the use of library materials in class work was limited in scope but quite revealing. It was to investigate the use by different sections of a large course of the books placed on reserve for that course. The course chosen was one in the department of history. A total of 247 students was enrolled in the course. Four instructors taught the several sections. All followed the same outline which involved the use of the same library reserves. This consisted of 293 volumes. A comparison of the reading done by the students working under the different instructors is shown in the table on the following page.

An examination of the grades given in these several sections shows no decided variation from the norm in any case. One should not attempt to generalize from this instance. But it does afford a perfect illustration of the looseness and carelessness with which many instructors regard the library aspects of their courses.[9]

[9]For fear lest Professor D in this series had either with or without authorization adopted a different set of reading materials for his students, the matter was taken up with him. He stated that he had followed the regular outline of the course which had been approved, but during the term had been extremely busy.

TABLE 21

READING DONE IN FOUR SECTIONS OF A HISTORY COURSE

Professor	No. of Students	Total Circulation	Av. Circulation per Student
A	51	898	17.50
B	94	778	8.25
C	33	332	9.50
D	69	12	.16

These studies have all come from one institution. Two facts argue strongly against their being regarded as local and atypical. The first is the fact that the instructors of this institution were trained at the same graduate schools as those of other American universities, and follow in general the commonly accepted methods of instruction. The second is the fact indicated in the previous chapter that the average number of books borrowed per student in this institution approximates so closely the figures found for other institutions.

These facts seem to give one explanation and probably the primary explanation of why students use the library so little. They do not use the library's books because in a great deal of their work they do not have to; they can do quite acceptable work, in some cases possibly better work, without doing so.

This does not deny or question the existence of courses in which the use of the library is absolutely essential to the work outlined, nor of professors who utilize its resources most effectively. One gets the impression from the data surveyed, however, that the library is a stage removed from the vital center of the work of teaching. The use of its resources, though highly recommended by all professors, is to a large extent a work of supererogation. A large number of teachers apparently could get along very well without extensive libraries, at least for the greater number of their students. If libraries are to be used only for their reference works, or for the researches of the faculty, or for certain special aspects of the instructional program, the facts should be plainly recognized and the institution developed along lines best suited to serve these ends. From the use made of them in undergraduate teaching, the case could be made that many colleges have better libraries than they need.

One comes back to this "removedness" of class room work from the library. What is it due to? Is it the physical separation of the books over in "the library," while teaching goes on elsewhere? Or does the primary factor lie in the nature of class organization of instruction which throws the emphasis inevitably upon the utterances of the sage in charge? One does not need to debate the issue between these or other alternatives. The fact which confronts one is that the library is not functioning in close and vital connection with the teaching program. The individuals responsible for this are the college president, who in the last analysis can be blamed for everything, the librarian, who has been content and at times desirous of running his show in his own way, and the faculty, who have in too many cases been willing to temper the wind to the shorn lamb. The ideational form in which this general academic inertia and possible misdirection has expressed itself has been the conception of the library as a depository of knowledge. Reservoirs of knowledge are highly needed and certain national and university libraries serve society greatly by performing this function. The college library can rarely and does not usually need to undertake this expensive role. Books in the library are useless unless they are used, and in a college this means primarily used for the teaching purpose for which the institution exists.

CHAPTER FOUR

Teaching with Books

THE FIGURES WHICH HAVE BEEN REVIEWED IN THE PRE-
vious discussions raise two questions, both of which
must be given serious consideration. The first of these
is a problem of objective. Should students use the library to an appreciably greater extent than at present?
The second is a practical matter. Can students be induced to do much more reading than at present?

To assert that intelligent and wisely directed reading is in general a desirable thing for those who are
students by occupation is merely to indulge in tautol-
ogy. Nor would many be disposed to deny that a certain amount of additional reading over and above
that usually accomplished would be profitable. Students like all the rest of us waste time, engage in activities which are unremunerative, and misdirect their
energies to a varying degree. Probably they err in
these respects more than other people, since most of
them are individuals experiencing for the first time
the joys of self-direction and acquiring only gradually the ability to choose those activities which yield
the greatest rewards. Anything which would help students to find themselves more quickly and surely, and
to substitute worth-while activities for wasteful and
purely frivolous ones is obviously desirable. With the
general problem of student guidance and character
development, however, we are not concerned at the
moment, though the obligation of the library to help
create an environment conducive to reading and
thought is clear enough. The immediate issue is a

more specific one, namely: is it desirable to stress more than at present the library or reading aspects of colleg teaching, recognizing that this will mean minimizing to a certain extent the emphasis which falls at present on oral instruction in organized classes? In other words, should the library play a fundamentally more important role in undergraduate education than it does in most institutions, and if so, what is that role?

When this question is sharply stated and seriously considered, it becomes evident that one will not meet with unanimous agreement as to the answer. There are a number of teachers and others who have come to feel that the "library method" has been overdone. A method of teaching which makes many assignments to books in the library has been criticized as expensive, wasteful of time, inevitably repetitious, and therefore dull and deadening to the student. In an article in the *Bulletin of the Association of American Colleges,* a librarian completed an analysis of the use of the library in college courses with the frank statement: "I have met a surprisingly large number of intelligent students who have expressed the opinion that required reading is an overworked fad of the present generation of teachers."[1] A similar opinion was recently expressed to the writer by an intelligent and productive scholar, who is believed to be a good teacher, in the statement that there is "a lot of bunkum about this library business." His method of instruction is to use from one to three texts, to lecture on the problems of international relations, and from time to time to cite additional materials which can be consulted in the library if the students wish to take the trouble. At least one college librarian can be cited who has been willing to put into print his conviction that the real function of the college library is to serve the community of scholars who compose the faculty, and

[1]Pierce Butler, "College Students Reading," *Bulletin of the Association of American Colleges,* XIX (1933), 345.

that those colleges which do not propose to encourage research work need only a small book collection.[2]

Such statements are warnings against easy assumptions as to the role of the library. The last thing that one would want to do would be to make a fetish of library circulation. Reading in many books rather than a few books is not always an intellectual gain. Two negative aspects, in particular, of this library problem must be kept in mind.

The first of these is the obvious fact that there are certain types of academic work which do not lend themselves readily to, or rather, do not really call for extensive library usage. Laboratory science courses and courses in mathematics have always been recognized as being of this sort. There are others of more varied classification in which this is equally true. Courses dealing with literary, religious, or philosophic classics might call for intensive or repeated reading of the particular work studied, rather than much reading about it in other volumes. Thinking, too, is better than reading, and there may be in a college curriculum courses in which the data are already familiar to the student and the task is to correlate and coordinate one's ideas and convictions. It is understandable that some courses of this sort might make little use of the library. Education can be gained in various ways, and no sensible person would urge a uniformity of teaching method irrespective of the subject matter involved. Nor would one wish to urge dispersion of attention and study where concentration and thoroughness are desired. The clear recognition of the existence of certain fields and of certain types of courses in other fields where the use of the library will be at least minimal is a necessary preliminary to any discussion of the problem of undergraduate library reading.

[2]T. E. Norton, "The College Library and College Teaching," *School and Society*, XLIII (February, 1936), 241-46.

A second point is equally obvious. One who watches the actual operation of most reserve book rooms where the volumes containing class assignments are handled soon becomes impressed with the fact that a considerable waste of time and effort is associated with the present practice, as well as a good deal of uncertainly on students' part concerning the various assignments. The exact contribution of the reading assigned to the course as a whole is not always clear. Frequently the assignments repeat each other and more frequently they repeat the class lectures. Uncertainty as to whether the assignment is to be read for its detailed information or for its general interpretation is a common difficulty. That which is essential for the understanding of the course and that which is less so is not always distinguished. The impression quoted above that "required reading is an overworked fad by the present generation of teachers," is sometimes easy to understand. It is by no means certain that an increased severity in checking up on reading requirements, if unaccompanied by a more careful planning of the latter, would constitute any great gain. The withdrawal and use of books in the library is a time- and energy-consuming operation at the best, and has no merit in itself. Unless the sections read have some specific contribution to make to the courses of study, such requirements involve misdirection of effort and loss of enthusiasm.

One phase of this confusion and student loss of time which is observable in the reserve book room calls for special mention. In nearly every college library one finds a certain number of courses in which the library is being called upon to supply textbooks for the students. Textbooks are books practically all of which must be read by the entire class. There seems to be little defense for throwing this burden on the library and little virtue in a heavy library circulation due to this cause. A system by which the textbooks are supplied by the library through the ordinary reserve book arrangements is expensive to the library, extremely inconvenient to the students, and has little defense on educational grounds. If a book is so important that it should be read virtually in its entirety by the whole class, it is wiser and fairer to expect this book to be bought by the students for their use and possession, or to be supplied by some rental plan. It will be necessary to return to this point later in the discussion of the reserve book room. At the moment the discussion is only concerned with emphasizing that not all library usage is admirable, and that some of it should be eliminated or modified rather than increased.

When all this has been said, however, one comes back to several basic facts about American undergraduate education. The following remarks are mostly platitudes, which only means that the judgments expressed rest on wide experience and general observation rather than on the opinion of the writer. The usual methods of instruction of American colleges, in which the emphasis is placed on the work in the class and on the use of one or more textbooks, have been recognized to be defective in certain particulars which are directly pertinent to the problem in hand.

1. Instruction by means of one or two textbooks read by the entire class and lectures addressed to the group provides a uniform fare for a group of students who will differ widely among themselves in background, acquaintance with the problems in hand and special interests in it. Furthermore, this uniform class fare is adjusted of necessity to the lower levels of student ability and interest. Since the final publication of the Pennsylvania study by Learned and Wood based on tests administered to nearly 45,000 students, the existence and importance of these differences have been placed beyond debate. A system of instruction which ignores the fact and continues to teach by

means of a uniform set of required readings is continuing beyond its usefulness and also beyond its necessity the methods of the secondary schools. In some way instruction must be adjusted to the individual to a somewhat greater degree than has been done, and this would seem to mean a use of a more varied and carefully described set of readings in the place of uniform assignments.

2. A method of teaching which rests essentially on a textbook to be discussed in class fails to introduce the student to the great literature of the subject. A textbook summarizing the present knowledge of a field is at times a great convenience. It may serve admirably as a guide or outline by which a subject can be organized. But as a substitute for a knowledge of those volumes which have been significant in the history of thought it may be compared with a capsule of chemical ingredients to be taken in place of a wholesome and appetizing meal. We have been slow in realizing this. As far back as 1880 Mr. Justin Winsor, librarian of Harvard College, wrote as follows: "I will not stop to discuss the thralldom, or if you choose, the practical necessity of the class system. It is quite true, however, that the arguments for it have resulted in the textbook—something that hits an average with a void on either side of it. I will not say that the library is the substitute of the textbook; but it is, I claim, its generous rival and abettor, helping where it fails and leading where it falters."[3] It was the same vigorous personality who pointed out that Henry James had "opened a new mine at Harvard when he led his students among the sources of history and directed them to do their own culling, and to make their own textbooks. He planted a new interest in the work and showed what a library is for."[4] In recent years

[3]"The College Library," Circulars of Information, No. 1 (Washington: U. S. Bureau of Education, 1880), p.8.
[4]Justin Windsor, "The College Library and the Classes," *Library Journal*, III (March, 1878), 5.

special efforts have been made in a number of leading colleges to get students to know the books on which our culture is founded rather than to learn about them. The curriculum of St. John's College, which is built on the principle that a knowledge and understanding of the one hundred most significant volumes is a liberal education, illustrates this tendency.

3. Closely related to this point is the familiar fact that a textbook and lecture system gives the student a one-sided view of the field of study. Faculty members who are keenly alert to the necessity of academic freedom to enable specialists to present views of public questions which may differ from those generally accepted, have not always been alert in avoiding a one-sided presentation of issues in their own courses. The presentation of the views of an opposing school in psychology, let us say, either in summary form in a text, or in a lecture planned to expose its weakness, is scarcely representative. The student has the right to be introduced to views other than those of his instructor, through the presentation of those who hold them. In all except the largest institutions this will have to be done by means of their published writings. A limitation of the work of the class to the works of one writer or group gives the student no sense of the movement of thought in the field, and thus fails to introduce him fairly to the subject of his study.

4. One of the most clearly recognized weaknesses of the present method of teaching is its tendency to divide the field of knowledge into small compartments which have little connection in the student's mind with each other. Efforts to overcome this departmentalization of knowledge have taken for the most part one of two forms. One plan utilizes one or more comprehensive examinations, by which it is hoped that the student will be required to integrate—as well as to retain—the knowledge previously acquired. A second approach has been the grouping of courses of

instruction into larger units, usually but by no means uniformly taken in the earlier college years.

This departmentalization of knowledge is much more than a library problem, but nevertheless its solution seems to involve a more extensive use of reading materials than the usual classroom method required. Unless the comprehensive examination is merely a review, it would seem to involve reading around specific courses and filling in gaps between them. The broader survey courses are intended to introduce the student to the major thinkers and influences in the area surveyed. No doubt textbooks will be written for these comprehensive survey courses, and the greater ease of teaching by this means will encourage their use. It is apparent, however, that thinness and superficiality can be avoided only by some direct contact or acquaintance, even to a limited degree, with the more important accomplishments in the field studied. Actual experience bears this out. Survey courses have in nearly every instance involved much more reading than the courses which they replaced.

5. There are several homely truths also which need to be kept in mind in considering whether a substantially greater emphasis on reading in college instruction is desirable. The first of these is that a knowledge of a large part of nearly every course can be secured not only as well but actually better from two or three standard volumes than from the lectures of the professor. There are, of course, topics on which the instructor should lecture, but there is a great deal on which lecturing is not necessary. The present system of class instruction tends to obscure this fact, indisputable as it is. A second practical consideration is the physical and mental strain of attending three or more lectures per day, each of fifty minutes duration, with laboratory work to be added in the afternoons. Few adults could stand this ordeal without mental and nervous exhaustion. Where instructors are good lec-

turers, the strain is no doubt less, but only a small per cent of college professors could make a living on the lecture platform. Lecturing is, of course, relieved to some extent by class discussion, but if the discussion involves topics adequately dealt with in the reading assigned, the case is no better. Regulations relieving the better students from class attendance and stopping all lecturing during a so called "reading period" indicate a growing realization that the lecture system has been overdone. A third practical point is the obverse of the latter. The college professor who takes his job seriously is—the public to the contrary—a very hard worked individual. In addition to his major responsibility, his teaching, he should engage in constant study or research, must serve on numerous committees, is frequently called upon to serve the local community, and occasionally the broader social interests. In addition to these duties it is highly desirable that he devote a certain amount of time to interviews with students and personal counsel of them in matters academic and otherwise. These practical points are all related to each other—the fact that a good part of the work of instruction need not be done by the expensive method of oral discourse, that constant attendance at lectures is exhausting and, except in the more favorable cases, destructive of zest and eagerness, and finally that time saved by faculty members for class sessions can be profitably devoted to other activities which are academically and socially valuable. They suggest that the answer to a number of academic problems is to be found in a greater emphasis on the reading aspect of college work.

As remarked, these criticisms of the traditional form of American college teaching are now generally recognized. The conventional method tends to make the student responsible to the course rather than to the subject matter of the field, to separate him from the literature of the subject, and to inculcate a deference to the authorities which have been set up, rather than to develop critical discernment and independent judgment. Modifications of the system, designed to secure a greater measure of responsibility and independence on the student's part and an adjustment of the program to the differences which exist between individuals, are being effected in many places. These newer educational devices are familiar enough and need not be detailed. They give the student more freedom, make him more responsible for his own education, and endeavor to test more adequately the progress he makes. This means that in place of specific assignments and set lectures, the student is directed to the literature of the subject, and the instructor becomes an aid in acquiring and understanding this knowledge rather than its source and final end.

The trend is thus plainly toward a greater use of books and related materials, rather than less. It is important to recognize that there are fundamental reasons for this, that the trend is not a concomitant of any particular educational device or fad. In some institutions tutorial systems or honors courses eliminate the class system entirely for those students permitted to do their work in this manner. In others the tutorial or individual reading course is only one element in the student's program. In still others the change of emphasis is accomplished within the usual form of class instruction, the instructor providing a clearer definition of the topics to be studied than usual, more adequate guidance to the literature dealing with them, and integrating carefully this reading and the work done in the class sessions. It appears probable that the forms of instruction will continue to vary: in contrast there seems general agreement that the student must acquire his own education, that the most obvious materials to be used by him are books and other reproductions of the world's thought and work, and that basically the teacher can only guide and assist the student's efforts toward self-education.

It appears thus that the most thoughtful educators have answered in the affirmative the question raised at the outset, Should students use books to an appreciably greater degree than at present? The small use made of college libraries in many institutions seems to indicate that to a large extent instruction rather than stimulation has been the guiding principle. The inevitable result of this has been a concern on the part of the students for meeting course requirements rather than for mastering the field of knowledge.

This brings up the second question stated at the outset of this chapter, Can one get college students to read extensively? The answer to this question is not in theoretical but in factual terms. Although the average number of loans to students has been seen to be depressingly low when the calculation is made on a sufficiently large basis, there are a number of institutions which have demonstrated that under certain conditions undergraduates will read much more heavily.

In the first place it must be recalled that the figures which were accepted above as norms for college use were averages based in a number of instances on groups of institutions. Separate figures for the colleges comprising these groups show that they differ markedly from each other and from the mean. In Waples' study of 35 colleges, in which the mean of 5.55 volumes per student per semester for the general collection was established, the institutional averages range from 1.8 to 16.35 loans per semester.[5] McDiarmid's 7 colleges showed a range from 11.46 titles per student per semester—general and reserve circulation combined—to 29.40 titles.[6] Mr. Johnson writes me that in the study he made of five colleges he found a similar variation between the several institutions.

[5]Douglas Waples, *et. al.*, *The Library* ("Evaluation of Higher Institutions," No. 4; Chicago: University of Chicago Press, 1936), p.55.
[6]E. W. McDiarmid, Jr.,"Conditions Affecting the Use of the College Library," *Library Quarterly*, V (1935), 64.

A more impressive answer to the question whether college students can be led to read extensively is supplied, however, by the special accomplishments in this respect of certain colleges. The evidence here is of two types. A number of institutions by the adoption of certain specific procedures have been able to bring about a marked increase in the use which their students make of their libraries, and presumably in the amount of reading which they do. In these cases comparisons with other institutions are not involved. In the case of certain other colleges dependable statistics make possible a comparison with the norms established above and indicate a noteworthy accomplishment from the standpoint of student reading. In certain cases both points are illustrated, and the two groups cannot be kept sharply apart. The point or points of special interest will be clear in each case from the data adduced.

Several points must be made very clear about these illustrations. In the first place it is not claimed that the colleges to be mentioned are doing a better job of education than others, but only that their students use more books from their libraries than is true in most cases. Any conclusions beyond this fact the reader must draw for himself. Nor is it even claimed that the greatest amount of student reading takes place in these colleges. These schools are mentioned merely because in their cases figures happened to be available in which the internal improvement or considerably greater than average use could be demonstrated.

1. In September 1931 Southwestern, a four year liberal arts college in Memphis, Tennessee, inaugurated a system of tutorial courses for all students above the freshmen level. For sophomores this course consisted of a half hour conference weekly with a tutor and approximately three hours per week of reading in one of the main divisions of the curriculum. In the

second semester the student elects a different division for this work, thus being introduced by this means to two of the six divisions. The object is to enable the student to discover his interests and talents. In the junior and senior years the student spends nine hours a week on his tutorial course, this taking the place of one of the regular courses formerly studied. Since June, 1936, general or comprehensive examinations in the major field of study have been instituted, the tutorial work being utilized also to fill in gaps between courses and otherwise to prepare the student for the examinations.

The merits of this particular program in contrast with other plans do not here concern us.[7] Its effect on student reading, however, cannot be questioned. The following circulation figures in which borrowings from the general collection and reserve book charges are combined, speak for themselves:

TABLE 22

CIRCULATION STATISTICS, SOUTHWESTERN, 1928-38

Year	No. of Vols. Withdrawn	No. of Students	No. of Withdrawals per Student
1928-29	19,099	415	46.02
1929-30	19,382	428	45.28
1930-31	22,247	417	53.35
1931-32	29,298	377	77.71
1932-33	27,851	370	75.29
1933-34	28,058	378	74.22
1934-35	27,839	353	78.86
1935-36	31,759	449	70.73
1936-37*	24,436	468	52.02
1937-38	25,070	489	51.20

*Only ten months, due to change in fiscal year, and rules changed from one week use of books to two weeks. The latter change applies also to 1937-38.

[7] Those interested in a study of the Southwestern tutorial plan, its results, difficulties and problems, will find this in the *Southwestern Bulletin*, n.s., XXII, Nos. 3 and 4 (October, 1935).

These figures were not gathered on the same basis as those presented in Chapter II. Daytime circulation of reserve books, for example, are not included, and there are other factors which differentiate the figures somewhat from the averages presented in Chapter II. They cannot be used therefore for purposes of comparison with other institutions. The series is consistent, however, and indicates a marked improvement in the use of the library as a result of the program instituted.

2. About ten years ago, Antioch College modified its course program by the adoption of what it called, "The Autonomous Plan." The essence of the plan was, according to the authorities, the shift of responsibility from the teacher to the student. The assumption was made that "the students were in college to secure an education, and that there would be available for their guidance a staff of experts in the various fields of knowledge and for their use adequate literary and laboratory facilities." The basis of each course was to be a carefully prepared syllabus, and the student was expected to proceed more or less independently of "assignments." A flexible plan of course instruction was substituted for the former rigid three-meetings-a-week system, introductory courses requiring more supervision than others. Attendance at class meeting is optional. For advanced students the plan is even more flexible, and "often the student under the guidance of the instructor prepares his own syllabus and takes the whole initiative." Comprehensive examinations covering both the required courses and the field of major interest are given. Some variation naturally exists among faculty members as to their skill in utilizing these provisions and the extent to which they followed. In a recent article in the *Educational Record,* President Henderson refers to two specific results of this program. One is the amount of individual faculty-student conference work which is

done. Quoting directly from this article, "Another is the larger role of the library in the task of instruction. Since 1929 (about the time of the introduction of the comprehensive examination and the autonomous study plan) the circulation of books in the library has nearly tripled, although the student enrollment has remained the same."[8]

The circulation figures for the period since the adoption of the autonomous plan are as follows:

TABLE 23

CIRCULATION STATISTICS, ANTIOCH COLLEGE, 1927-38

Year	No. of Stu-dents	Book Circula-tion	Periodi-cal Circu-lation	Av. Book Charges per Student	Av. Total Charges per Student
1927-28	706	14,826	1,259	21.0	22.78
1928-29	664	14,138	1,219	21.3	23.13
1929-30	680	17,515	1,178	25.7	27.49
1930-31	640	22,868	1,015	35.7	37.32
1931-32	601	25,658	1,823	42.7	45.65
1932-33	568	30,925	1,707	54.4	57.45
1933-34	561	34,623	2,480	61.7	66.14
1934-35	624	36,391	2,788	58.3	62.79
1935-36	668	36,558	2,212	54.7	58.04
1936-37	701	34,499	2,912	49.2	53.37
1937-38	680	39,019	2,909	57.3	61.66

The Antioch College Library is administered almost entirely on an open shelf basis, which makes the recorded circulation the more significant. The reserved books, for example, are freely accessible, and the only figures gathered for them are the overnight withdrawals. Less than a third of the total recorded circulation was of these reserved books. For several reasons therefore these figures cannot be used for comparative purposes, but are consistent within the series.

[8]A. D. Henderson, "Individualization in the Antioch Program," *Educational Record,* XIX, Supplement 11 (January, 1938), 49f.

3. During a four year period from 1930-31 to 1933-34 the per student use of the general collection at Lawrence College doubled, while the use of the reserve collection also showed a small increase. Although the latter year was the peak of the circulation figures, the decline since then has not been a significant one. The following figures give the total recorded circulation for these years, it being impossible now to distinguish between student and non-student loans. They are not to be used therefore for comparative purposes:

TABLE 24

CIRCULATION STATISTICS, LAWRENCE COLLEGE, 1930-34

Year	No. of Students	Regular Circulation	Reserve Circulation	Av. Regular Circulation per Student	Av. Reserve Circulation per Student
1930-31	751	15,830	24,568	21.0	32.7
1931-32	698	18,486	22,797	26.5	32.7
1932-33	675	24,860	24,680	36.8	36.5
1933-34	636	27,602	26,280	43.4	41.3

Inquiry as to the causes of this improvement reveals no single factor as responsible. A problem of library space led to a conscious effort to keep down the number of reserve books. At the same time a tutorial plan was adopted and the faculty was urged to reduce the number of textbooks used and depend more upon a wider range of reading. Interest in the library led also to efforts to speed up the purchase of books and to keep the collection fresh and interesting by the addition of new volumes. President Wriston modestly writes: "I have always felt that no one factor alone accounted for the change. It was a combination of small items which produced the result." From all the data that can be secured it would appear to an outsider that the fundamental factor was simply that the work of the library was given serious consideration by the administrative authorities of the college and attention given to the various problems which this raised.

4. A few years ago Mr. Joseph Brewer, an Oxford University graduate, found himself engaged in the reorganization of Olivet College. Drawing upon his own experience he reorganized the curriculum in such a way that there were few regular classes after the freshman year, the remainder of the work being done largely by individual direction. In the library the following results were noted: the total reading of the students increased, the reserve book usage declined, and the reference work of the librarians increased greatly. Circulation figures from 1934, the last year of the old system, run as follows, all nonstudent loans being excluded:

TABLE 25

CIRCULATION STATISTICS, OLIVET COLLEGE, 1934-39

Year	No. of Students	Regular Circulation	Reserve Circulation	Av. Regular Circulation per Student	Av. Reserve Circulation per Student
1934-35	202	5,147	24,849	25.48	123.0
1935-36	252	7,768	16,829	30.8	66.8
1936-37	258	12,573	15,865	48.3	61.5
1937-38	272	13,448	18,056	49.4	66.4
1938-39	263	17,601	12,058	66.8	45.8

Thus within four years the average number of withdrawals per student from the general collection more than doubled, though at the same time the reserve usage declined to a similar degree. No one familiar with reserve book reading, particularly where it is the fashion to make a number of very short specific assignments, will doubt that this represents a very substantial increase in reading. The testimony of the librarian on this point is as follows:

> In adjusting the library to the new plan of education there was not so much to do as one might expect. The only difficulty lay in getting used to the fact that students really were interested in doing some individual work. . . . The change has meant a greater real demand for the books on hand and also for books not on hand. It has meant a greater interest in the library and library affairs on the part of every one. . . . Students come with all sorts of questions and we want to help them find the information they need. When the library merely supplied the books assigned and once in a while the material for a paper, we had an easy but dull time of it. Now we must be up on our toes every minute, ready to advise and assist in collecting material on all sorts of topics.[9]

The careful exclusion of all nonstudent reading from the Olivet figures makes it possible to compare these averages with the norms set forward in Chapter II. It will be noted that the 1938-39 reserved book circulation is slightly less than the figure of 50 to 60 indicated there, while the Olivet general circulation average is more than five times that shown for the colleges considered in that chapter.

5. In these instances the emphasis has fallen on the improvement which the colleges have been able to bring about in the amount of reading done by their students, though in the last case it was also possible to use the figures for comparative purposes. In the case of the two institutions to be cited next the point of interest is a comparison with the averages established in Chapter II. Both are small colleges which emphasize individual instruction and student self-responsibility in study. Both have relatively small book collections. Both illustrate the extent to which stu-

[9]From an unpublished paper read at the Michigan Library Association annual meeting, October 18, 1935, by Miss Mary Hammond.

dents will use the library where the curriculum and method of instruction is planned with that expectation. These two were selected for special attention because their methods of instruction emphasized reading and because it was found that some—though not all—of the desired data could be easily secured. No doubt both of them possess certain advantages, but the same advantages found elsewhere are not in every instance accompanied by special interest in reading on the part of students.

Bennington College was established in 1932 on the basis of certain well defined educational convictions. Among these were the following:

That the college should accustom its students to the habit of engaging voluntarily in learning rather than of submitting involuntarily at certain periods to formal instruction;

That external disciplines, such as compulsory class attendance, competitive and publicly awarded grades and prizes, periodic written examination on formalized blocks of knowledge, and numerical accumulation of credits to earn degrees, interfere seriously with real incentives and internal disciplines related to the students' own developing purposes and interests.

That progress of college work should at all points allow for the fact that between different students and in the same student at different times, there is wide individual variation as to subject matter and problems which have meaning and will therefore engage the student in active learning leading to understanding.[10]

With the various forms in which Bennington College has endeavored to give expression to these ideals, this discussion will not deal. Some of them without doubt are related to its own particular problems and may or may not be applicable elsewhere. The general objectives, however, so clearly imply as one of the

[10]*Bennington College Bulletin*, VI, No. 1 (August, 1937), 6ff.

bases of the college program the expectation that students will forward their education by the constant use of books and other printed materials, that the college becomes an experiment in how much may be expected along these lines.

The following figures are not total circulation records. They represent student borrowings only. Faculty and other loans have been excluded. Furthermore, it should be noted that they are the borrowings for the academic year only, loans to the small summer school being excluded. The Bennington Library furthermore has open stacks and a self-charging system. The figures below do not represent therefore a meticulous counting of every time a book is looked at, which one sometimes encounters. Lastly, it should be remembered that the Bennington students are resident on the campus for only 30 weeks in the year. For the first two years of the library's work accurate figures are not available. For the period from 1934 to date the circulation has been as follows:

TABLE 26

CIRCULATION STATISTICS, BENNINGTON COLLEGE, 1934-38

Year	No. of Students	Regular Circulation	Reserve Circulation	Av. Regular Circulation per Student	Av. Reserve Circulation per Student
1934-35	221	13,229	3,309	59.9	14.9
1935-36	250	15,257	3,245	61.0	13.0
1936-37	266	15,449	3,155	58.0	11.8
1937-38	278	15,489	3,655	55.7	13.1

In appraising these figures one should recall that the averages reached in Chapter II of about 12 volumes per year per student from the general collection and 50 to 60 charges with about half that number of titles from the reserved book collection were secured under

closed shelf conditions. The Bennington figures, secured for a shorter academic period,[11] and under open
shelf free access and self-charging conditions, reverses
these figures for the general circulation and the reserves. There is of course no accurate way to equate
the use of books under the limitations of reserved
book rules and books loaned for two weeks. Most librarians feel that the latter are far more significant.
Estimating simply on the basis of titles used, the
Bennington figures are about 55 per cent higher than
the general average. Taking into consideration the
open shelf conditions and the shorter period of resi-
dency and other factors, it is obvious that the amount
of reading done will exceed the general average by
considerably more than that amount. No mathematical ratio, however, can be set down.

6. Across the continent from Bennington is Reed
College in Oregon. A coeducational college of moderate size it has recently celebrated its twenty-fifth anni-
versary. While no longer an experimental college, it
has become known for its insistence upon small classes
and its emphasis on student self-responsibility. Comprehensive examinations are given sophomores and
seniors. Seniors must write a thesis representing a good
deal of independent work under faculty direction.
The library is operated on the open shelf principle
with the exception of a portion of the books placed
on reserve. In this instance, owing to a change in the
way in which the records have been preserved, I am
able to cite the figures for only one year. From these
figures summer school loans, loans to faculty members
and to other individuals have been excluded. This
will explain the much larger figures which have been
published elsewhere for this institution. The figures
are for the academic year, 1937-38. One notes that the

---

[11]Practically no books are taken home by the students during the
two months' winter field and reading period. In 1936-37 the student
borrowing for this period numbered 38 volumes.

average number of loans from the general collection is nearly four times the figure which has been used as a norm, while the reserve book charges remain at the upper limit of the norm.

No. of Students	General Circula- tion	Average per Student	Reserve Circula- tion	Average per Student
484	22,500	46.48	30,066	61.91

Before proceeding further with the discussion, one may be permitted a further word as to the factors responsible for the success of the institutions discussed in securing a better than average use of books on the part of their students or a marked increase over previous rates. In certain instances plainly and in all instances no doubt a variety of influences were at work. Nevertheless a common feature which runs through all these cases has been the modification to some degree of the traditional system of instruction. In each of the colleges mentioned one finds efforts on the one hand to discover the individual with his special difficulties and interests, and on the other hand to shift in some part the responsibility to the individual for his own education. This is no proof that such newer modes of education are better. But it does show that students will read, if the institution makes it clear that it really regards this as of fundamental importance.

Partly lest the above discussion should seem to be special pleading, partly because the institution deserves mention in this connection for its own sake, I cite next a college in which a marked increase in the use of the library has been secured in connection with the ordinary forms of teaching. The institution is Stephens College, a junior college for women in Columbia, Missouri. The institution needs to be visited to be understood. It lays much emphasis on the educational value of student activities and a cultural environment. As part of the latter it has provided dormitory libraries and personal collections to be retained in their rooms by students. The teaching program emphasizes personal consultation and guidance, but has not modified in any striking way the organization of instruction in regular classes. Certain courses are exceptions to this statement. A course in the masterpieces of literature, for example, directs individual reading according to the background, interests and other special needs of the student. The only sessions of this class are held in the library reading rooms. The college has, however, emphasized in various ways the importance of books in the work of teaching. The librarian, Mr. B. Lamar Johnson, is also dean of instruction, and classroom teaching and the library are thus linked together. Book collections are provided in a considerable number of classrooms and departmental offices. Two divisional libraries, one for social sciences and one for the natural sciences, have librarians who do some teaching in these fields. This program was begun in 1932. Table 27, the circulation for the years since that date, with the two previous years for comparison, is presented. From the years 1933-34 to date all nonstudent loans have been excluded. For the first three years the materials for doing this were not available. Judging by these subsequent years this would reduce the general circulation averages from two to three volumes for each of the years 1930-33, and make the improvement achieved even more than is indicated.

It will be noted that this emphasis on the importance of the library and its use at Stephens College has resulted in more than doubling the circulation in five years. The figures since 1933-34 can be compared with those which have been used as norms. Although the reserved book circulation average is much less than the average indicated in Chapter II, the general circulation is nearly three times the average used as the norm. If an effort is made to reduce these two

TABLE 27

CIRCULATION STATISTICS, STEPHENS COLLEGE, 1930-38

Year	No. of Students	General Circulation		Reserve Book Circulation		Total Circulation per Student
		No.	Per Student	No.	Per Student	
1930-31	624	7,487	12.00	1,538	2.46	14.46
1931-32	618	8,797	14.44	1,448	2.34	16.78
1932-33	485	10,250	25.28	1,146	2.36	27.64
1933-34	610	14,921	24.46	2,286	3.75	28.21
1934-35	740	26,094	35.26	3,412	4.61	39.87
1935-36	874	26,884	30.75	4,147	4.84	35.59
1936-37	914	27,219	29.77	4,451	4.87	34.64
1937-38	1,167	39,442	33.79	7,446	6.38	40.17

types of usage to a common term on the basis of titles used—the reserved charges being assumed to be about twice the number of titles withdrawn—the Stephens average would be about equal to the norm. Because of the open shelf arrangement of much of the Stephens book collection, the figures listed in the table do not tell all of the story. It must be remembered furthermore that Stephens is a junior college and that the heaviest reading is generally expected in the upper academic years. It would appear, therefore, that the institution can be cited not only as one which has achieved a marked increase in the reading of its students, but also a per student use which is better than the average.

The above cases indicate the results which certain institutions have achieved when they have given serious attention to the question of student self-education by means of books. They do not, let it be repeated, represent a complete list of all colleges which have secured such results, but are only cases in which definite figures could be secured to demonstrate the point. The lack of such figures in a number of instances was especially regretted. One would have particularly liked,

77

for example, to have been able to see the effect on student reading of the introduction of the "honors courses" at Swarthmore College or, as an alternative, a statistical statement of the amount of reading done at present under this system. The lack of comparable circulation records throughout the period involved prevented the former, and the open shelf conditions of the library and, more particularly, the absence of any distinction between loans to undergraduates and to other borrowers blocked the latter. There was unanimous agreement, however, of all observers consulted that the per student use of the library under the present system greatly exceeded the rate before the introduction of the honors courses.

Similar difficulties prevented an appraisal of the effect of the full development of the "four course plan" at Princeton on undergraduate use of the library. When this plan, which calls for individual programs of work under faculty guidance in the junior and senior years, in lieu of the fifth course, was first instituted, an immediate increase in library circulation was observed. I quote from the report of the librarian for the year 1923-24:

The recorded use of the Library has shown a most striking and gratifying increase during the past year, the total being 131,507 as against 96,887 in 1922-23 and 86,760 in 1920-21. I have no doubt but that the largest influence, determining this increase, is the new course of study. There has been an increase in practically every one of the elements of our circulation. About 9,000 more were loaned for one- and two-week periods. Approximately the same number of books were reserved for class use at the desk, but these books have been used 12,000 more times than last year.

The number of registered graduate and undergraduate borrowers of books has increased from 1842 last year to 2172 this year; or, expressed in another way, last year 80 per cent of the students borrowed books for use in their rooms and this year 90 per cent.

While the circulation at Princeton has continued to show a steady increase it has not been possible to isolate the undergraduate use for special discussion.

The effect on the library usage of the Chicago "College Plan" has been described in Boucher's volume[12] and by Mr. Raney, the librarian.[13] Both observers were confident that the careful planning of the new courses and the emphasis placed on reading assignments rather than lectures, had resulted in greatly increased reading. Owing to the amount of this supplied in textbooks and rental sets, and to the number of libraries available to these students, the circulation figures of the college library are not a complete index. Since a special study of the use of this college library is now being made by Mr. G. Donald Smith, a fellow in the Graduate Library School, it seems the part of wisdom to await its results rather than to attempt any estimate of the effect of this widely discussed plan.[14]

Although much can be done to encourage and increase student reading by making books easily and attractively accessible and by other means, it is plain that the fundamental question in this connection is the character of the instructional work of the college. Books bought by the library lie unused on the shelves because instructors in large numbers are not depending upon these volumes to supply any essential element in the educational processes for which they are

[12]C. S. Boucher, *The Chicago College Plan* (Chicago: University of Chicago Press, 1935), p.181ff.

[13]M. L. Raney, "The New College Plan at the University of Chicago and Its Library," *Library Journal,* LIX (1934), 193-96.

[14]Boucher published the following figures: In 1931-32 the average number of book withdrawals per registrant in the humanities and the social science survey courses was 67 volumes; in 1932-33 it was 76.94 and in 1933-34 it was 79.96. It must be remembered that these were mostly of the short period or reserved book character. Raney in his article gives an average of 62 for all 1500 students enrolled in the college. These figures, however, are not much above the combined general and reserved book averages established in Chapter II.

responsible. The library will be used heavily only when books become the major instruments by which the educational program is carried on. The basic reasons for believing that this type of teaching is desirable to a far greater extent than at present are not merely ones of economy or educational novelty, but certain clearly defined educational ends or objectives which the traditional technique plainly fails to achieve. (This throws the ultimate responsibility back on the college administration as a whole to formulate and clarify the ultimate educational objectives which it seeks. Upon the individual instructor, however, the task finally devolves. This means that the problem of the library calls for a clear appraisal and agreement of the college body as a whole on the ends of education and the part which reading and study should play in the process, and a unified endeavor to carry this out.)

But if the library is to become to a greater extent than heretofore the instrument of education, it must become more clearly aware of its task and more concerned with it. The integration of the library and the work of instruction cannot take place entirely from one side. The changing status of the library in the total educational picture calls for coordinate changes in library practice and policy. The remainder of this volume will address itself to some of the more important issues which the library must face in any effort to achieve this integration.

CHAPTER FIVE

Some Responsibilities
of the College President

WHAT KIND OF LIBRARY DOES THE COLLEGE NEED IF A greater emphasis is going to be placed on self education and the use of books either in connection with normal classroom work or with some of the newer educational devices? To answer that question it is necessary to state in a more systematic form than has been done the functions which this college library must perform.

Primarily, under present conditions, the college library is a service agency. This fact devolves from the general form of colleges in which a faculty of subject specialists is employed to be primarily responsible for the work of instruction. The library's duty, therefore, is to aid this faculty in its work, providing in large part a means for their work and enabling students to carry on the courses of study which are recommended or prescribed. The college library is thus not an end in itself. In this respect it differs from the national libraries and from the research libraries which, in part at least, in their endeavors to preserve knowledge in great book collections are ends in themselves. The college library has the same *raison d'être* as the college of which it is a part, it exists for the sake of teaching or educating undergraduate students. The primary responsibility for the direction of this educational process, however, will always rest with the faculty.

Several general obligations or aspects of this task are clearly discernible:

1. To provide the books, periodicals and related

materials needed in connection with this educational program.

2. To provide conveniently arranged and reasonably comfortable physical facilities for study, such as reading rooms, carrels, private desks, etc.

3. To study the part which the use of books plays in the educational work of the college and the occasions and conditions of their use, in order to devise ever more effective ways of facilitating this use by student and faculty member. In this respect the librarian is a tactician, deploying his books as does a military commander his varied forces.

4. To provide students with direction, guidance and aid in study regarding where information may be found, what books to read for particular purposes, etc., in so far as this may be necessary. The extent to which the library will be called upon to exercise this function will vary in different institutions, depending largely on the character of the teaching. It is, however, present and necessary to some degree in every college library.

The fundamental function of the library is thus to forward, rather than to originate, the educational program of the campus. It must provide the materials recommended, must remove so far as is possible all barriers between them and the students, and must facilitate the flow of suggestion from class lecture, conference and syllabus to book contacts and book use. It is not only the connecting link between teaching and learning, but where students are intelligent and inquisitive the library can supplement from its rich resources what the classroom has failed to supply.

This service to students in cooperation with the instructional program is certainly the main job of the college library. Around this central obligation is a fringe of other duties. These include the provision and recommendation of books of general and recreational character, aid to faculty members in research, the preservation of local annals and some rare books, book service to alumni, and a number of other duties. As useful and important as some of these are, they are not the main job.

This point, as indisputable as it seems to be, has not always been clearly perceived. The multiplicity of worthwhile services which a college library can render has obscured in the minds of many librarians the primacy of this duty of aiding the work of instruction. While all librarians would agree that it is their duty to provide and circulate books needed in the courses of study, a good many of them are inclined to feel, if not to maintain, that their responsibility along these lines ends with these activities. They are fearful lest any more positive attitude would be resented as unwarranted interference. Their educational task has been viewed rather along lines of general or recreational reading, and to the encouragement and development of this type of reading they have given much attention and enthusiasm. More than one librarian has expressed to the writer the belief that what really "counts" in the case of college students is voluntary reading, not that which is required in connection with course work. In this one sees partly the effect of the public library, partly the expression of a commendable zeal for books which has been given little outlet in most colleges in connection with the courses of study. Practice ofttimes follows this general principle. In visiting the libraries one sees many exhibits of books for recreational reading, current fiction, biographies, travel books and the like. One often sees displays of new books of general interest. I have yet to see an exhibit of books of interest to students in connection with any course of study. The reply that the course readings set up by the faculty constitute the exhibits in these cases is not quite adequate in view of the possibilities of added attractiveness and interest which a capable and interested librarian would often see in such shelves. Yet, after all, the college is built around the courses of study, and it is usually assumed that students come to college for the sake of the curriculum. At any rate, when students fail to do satisfactory work in connection with these courses we ask them to leave. Recreational reading in such a situation, where reading is the main job, has in fact a less important part to play than in other situations where one's daily task calls for activity of a different sort. There are certain definite services which non-curricula reading can render, and these will be discussed in another connection. They are, however, secondary ones and the librarian is running a counter show, if his or her interest and resources are thrown behind a current literature shelf to the neglect of the more serious interests on which the college stakes its existence. The college librarian has a different task from his colleague in the public library.

The college president is ultimately responsible for the conduct and character of the library. If he would secure the fullest educational returns from his college library, there are three specific services which he must render it, besides providing adequate financial support. These are (a) to take the lead in clarifying in the minds of all concerned the kind of library program which the college wants, (b) to select the librarian qualified to direct that service, and (c) to see to it that in the organization of the college the librarian is not separated from, but rather is brought into vital relationship to, the educational program. In most colleges this will mean elevating the status of the librarian.

The first of these is so obvious as to call for little comment or elaboration. It was remarked in the first chapter of this study that one of the most certain needs of the college library was to develop a distinctive program of its own. The great research libraries on the one hand and the public libraries on the other, particularly in the light of the prestige of the former and the fact that most of the faculty members have been trained in them, have tended to confuse and obscure the essential function of the college library. The latter has attempted to a certain degree to be all things to all men. The president owes it to his librarian to be clear in his own mind as to the type of library administration he wants and is prepared to support. This involves frankly facing such questions as the possibility of greater book losses with open shelf arrangements, control of duplication in book buying, as well as other issues. Librarians, as usually selected, are likely to carry out the general policy which the administration of the college wants. If the latter has no policy but merely wants "a library," it cannot complain if the librarian has none, or develops one on the basis of convenience of library administration. This is not a plea for an oracular utterance from the president's office, but rather for a realization of the educational importance of the way in which the library is conducted, and for administrative leadership in securing common agreement on a policy for it. An illustration of the contribution to library effectiveness of this interest on the part of the college president was cited in the previous chaper, that of Lawrence College. President Wriston's convictions on the subject of the library, expressed in many articles in library journals and elsewhere, have made a contribution far beyond the limits of his own campus. It is not unreasonable to attribute largely to his consistent interest the increase in the use of the Lawrence College Library which has been described. To cite negative instances, in which librarians struggling with difficult problems of relationship and policy, have become discouraged by lack of interest on the part of the college president in anything except how much it costs, would not be evidence of any elaborate research.

The second contribution to library effectiveness for which the president is responsible is the selection of a well qualified and competent librarian. This is at present a most difficult task. For librarianship, having made the mistake of emphasizing routines and techniques rather than intellectual interests and educational insight—a trend in which college administrators have for the most part acquiesced—finds itself unable to supply in sufficient numbers the more broadly qualified individuals whom the colleges are beginning to demand.

What are the qualifications which the job demands? Before answering, the point must be made again that this study deals with the college and not the university library. The duties of the librarians of the respective institutions are largely identical, but with a very definite change of emphasis. The university librarian, having under him a staff of from 25 to 200 individuals and being responsible for expenditures which run into the hundreds of thousands of dollars annually, must have marked administrative abilities. The administrative task of the college librarian is comparatively a simple one. The technical problems of a university library are far more complex and intricate, though this is to a certain extent balanced by the presence on the university library staff of specialists in library techniques. The bibliographic knowledge of the university librarian and his acquaintance with foreign, scientific and scholarly literature must also be much more recondite than that of his college colleagues. On the other hand, the college librarian will have more contacts with students and with individual faculty members than will the university librarian. The university post, in other words, makes more of a demand for the qualities of an administrator, organizer and bibliographer; the college position more of the qualities of the teacher and educator. With this distinction in mind one can set out three main qualifications for the college librarian besides those general ones of intelligence and integrity which would be assumed. These are (a) a knowledge of the principles of library administration, (b) scholarly interests and understanding, with which is included an interest in the education of college undergraduates, and (c) an ability to work with students and to cooperate smoothly and efficiently with those sometimes difficult individuals, the faculty. Each of these calls for some special comments.

Obviously, the librarian must know or acquire quickly the general principles of library administration. During its more than half a century of existence the library profession has acquired a considerable body of organized experience. There is no need for librarians to go over the painful road of experimentation which is evident in the professional literature of the closing decades of the last century. The present methods of cataloging and classification and of the organization of the library staff do not appear to be the final ones, but it would be foolish to attempt to work out new and original systems without reference to this accumulated body of experience. The librarian must know not only the technical processes of library administration, but also the major reference and professional tools, such as the trade and subject bibliographies, and the catalogs in book and card forms of the great book collections of the world. He needs to know something about book binding and book repair work, to which one might now add a working knowledge of microphotography. These technical matters constitute a body of professional knowledge which no librarian nowadays can be without. It is not, however, a profound body of knowledge, comparable for example to knowledge of the ancient world, the science of mathematics, or of chemistry. The generally accepted training which is regarded as essential for library work is a nine months' course taken by one holding a creditable A.B. degree. Advanced training leading to a master's degree in library science or to the doctorate is now offered, and it can scarcely be doubted that such training is profitable. That it is essential, however, is questioned by many librarians as well as other observers.

The possession of a broad cultural background, a knowledge of scholarly objectives and methods, and an interest in education is quite as vital to the successful performance of the duties of the college librarian as is technical professional knowledge, but has been more often ignored by those making the selection. And yet the necessity of it should be obvious. Members of the college faculty are scholars and scientists, and one who is to be their colleague must be not only appreciative of scholarship but also able to understand its methods, both in teaching and in research. Without this basic understanding the librarian and the faculty will speak different languages, and always be more or less at odds with each other. One will not have to wait long for difficulties to begin to appear. The probable result of the appointment of a librarian whose outlook is merely technical and clerical will be an over-emphasis on the importance of these procedures and an administration which will appear to the faculty to be hampering at many points. Voluntary efforts beyond the range of the librarian's real understanding and judgment, are too likely to result in difficulties, which will lead to a loss of initiative and a negative attitude toward all new proposals. On the other hand, a librarian with the cultural and educational qualifications referred to would not only be able to do a better job in the library, but also can be of inestimable value in college councils. Most colleges need badly in such councils individuals of scholarly outlook, who know the curriculum and who know students, but who represent no departmental interest.

The third qualification is usually recognized and

does not call for elaboration. It is rooted in the statement that the library is essentially a service agency, though it has its own distinctive contributions to make. The library, of all institutions on the campus, cannot be self-centered in its interests, and the librarian must recognize this. At the same time, he is responsible for a service to the whole community and must be able to refuse a request if it would result in poorer service. The librarian is like the head of the commissary department of the army. Without its work the army would disintegrate, but the officer in charge will scarcely become the national hero. To serve in this role requires intelligence, tact, and imagination. Above all, the librarian must think in terms of the college program as a whole and the ultimate end it is trying to achieve, and draw his inspiration and reward from its total contribution. For in details he must be guided constantly by others, and his daily services will not appear remarkable. Consistently and intelligently carried out, however, they add up to a distinguished educational service, but the librarian must be willing to wait for his rewards. The elements of character or disposition which enter into such an attitude and bearing are difficult to analyze and isolate, but the quality of mind and character involved is an indispensable factor for the most successful performance of the duties of the post.

The three general qualifications sketched above are all essential, but, unfortunately, in most individuals they are present in varying degrees. In view of this likelihood, it may not be amiss to remark that if one had to choose between technical proficiency and scholarly qualities of mind, it would seem wiser to choose the latter. The grounds for such a decision would be the principle that it is easier to add technical training to scholarship than scholarship to technical training. Given the scholarly outlook and training and the proper personal qualifications—among which a decent humility stands very high—the technical training can be acquired either by attendance at library school, or by assiduous study of the literature, along with practical experience. Such an appointee may make some mistakes in the early years of his service, but they will not add up to so expensive a total as those of a librarian who through many years of service will never be able to enter fully into the essential undertakings of the college. Of this general truth the leaders of the library profession are now keenly aware. In discussing the question of recruiting, a recent chairman of the Board of Education for Librarianship of the American Library Association made the following statement:

The Board is emphatically and uncomprisingly resolved that the requirements for those seeking admittance to professional education should center upon the quality of their previous liberal arts education. Indeed the most crying need in the library profession today is probably that of well educated rather than technically trained workers.[1]

Similarly, Mr. Ralph Munn, Director of the Carnegie Library of Pittsburgh, in a recent essay sums up the matter: "Successful librarianship is to a great extent dependent upon (a) general education with special emphasis upon a wide knowledge of books, (b) common sense and other personal traits, and (c) a relatively small amount of special library technique."[2]

Should the college librarian have the Ph.D. degree? The question is raised only because it has been put many times. College presidents, of all people, should be immune to the lure of academic trappings. Degrees no more than clothes make the man. After an introductory period on a college campus a man rates per-

[1]Adam Strohm, "The Platform of the Board of Education for Librarianship," *Bulletin of the Association of American Colleges,* XIII (1927), 235.
[2]Ralph Munn, *Conditions and Trends in Education for Librarianship* (New York: The Carnegie Corporation of New York, 1936), p.17.

haps more nearly for his own worth than in most situations. If the question be posed in the form, Should the college librarian be a specialized scholar, the answer must be carefully made. What is demanded of the librarian from the standpoint of scholarship is an understanding of research methods, a wide general knowledge, particularly as regards books, an ability to use French and German, and an interest in educational procedures and results. Specialized scholarship in a particular field will not be nearly so useful to the college librarian as these more general qualifications. But given these qualities, further mastery of a special field of study can only be regarded as an additional asset, which will aid the librarian in many ways and enrich the intellectual life of the community.[3]

This general answer to the question has been disputed on the ground that if the librarian is to work effectively with a group of scholars, he should have a scholarly training the equal of theirs. The danger in this view would seem to be that it demands of the librarian an equipment not only comparable to that of the faculty, but of the same character. His work, however, is radically different in one respect. An appointee to a professional chair must be an expert in one particular field; the librarian's work covers the entire range of the curriculum. His excellence and ultimately his standing among his colleagues will be determined by the skill and efficiency with which he can function in this broader task. One group of professional leaders meet this difficulty with the recommendation that the future librarian should attain the doctorate in the field of librarianship itself, a considerable amount of work in related fields such as education and sociology being required. Whether the

[3]In connection with this discussion the writer is reminded of a small detail in a many-figured pattern of paternal advice: "Never marry a girl, my son, because she has money; but if she happens to have some, don't hold that against her."

principles and practices of librarianship constitute a
sufficiently comprehensive body of knowledge to warrant a doctorate in the field, turns on a definition of
the meaning of that degree, and is a debate into
which this discussion need not enter. It is enough to
note that this plan of library training recognizes that
it is important for a librarian to know a great deal
besides library techniques and also that a specialized
knowledge of a subject field is not essential.[4]

It is easier to describe an ideal librarian than it is
to find one who is looking for a job. The natural
sources of supply are of course the library schools and
other libraries in which younger workers will have secured practical experience. Partly because of low salaries, partly because the profession has emphasized
routine practices more than educational objectives,
there have not been attracted a sufficient number of
individuals of the sort described to supply the demand. The situation is undoubtedly improving, but
many college administrators, eager for a librarian able
to make a distinctive contribution to the teaching program, have had difficulties in finding their man. If
the above analysis of the librarian's qualifications be
sound, there is no reason why in such cases of difficulty some recruiting for the profession should not be
undertaken. "It is evident," reads the report of the
Committee convened in April 1933 by the Carnegie
Corporation to study trends in education for librarianship, "that the library school is not the only means
of approaching librarianship. Many of the most influential leaders of the day were not so trained; and
it is reasonable to suppose the time will not soon come

[4]There is a large literature on the subject of training for librarianship, and any thorough discussion of the question would require a
more detailed study of the topic than the present writer can claim.
The interested reader is particularly recommended to examine the
pamphlet referred to above, *Conditions and Trends in Education for
Librarianship*, by Ralph Munn, which contains a discussion of a
number of important issues by experts who have followed closely the
development of library schools.

when the school will be the only door through which to enter the profession. The exceptional man in work requiring broad knowledge and an inquiring mind will always find his way over the mountains. One of the strong features of library service is this very unusual possibility of attracting outstanding material."[5] Able college librarians have been drawn repeatedly from other occupations. The most obvious hunting ground, however, has been among the ranks of the teaching profession. How satisfactory is this source of supply? Does the college professor make a good librarian?

To this question, in its general form, there seems to be only one answer. The academic training and experience of the college teacher would supply, so far as it goes, an ideal preparation for the job. It is sometimes objected that the faculty member's special interest in one field would make him partial to this aspect of the book collection. One knows of cases where this has happened, but in such instances it is not the special knowledge which is at fault, but a lack of balance and judgment. College presidents are usually recruited from the teaching profession without any such dire results being the rule.

The college professor who transfers his work to the library will have to acquire a knowledge of library procedures and management. This knowledge is not born in the classroom. Knowledge of Elizabethan England will not enable a man to decide whether a book should be bound by machine sewing or sewn through the signatures, nor will a familiarity with the classical world provide much help in deciding whether the library should adopt a different scheme of classification. The quickest and surest way to secure this training would be by attendance at one of the library schools during one or more summer sessions or for part of an academic year. At present there are difficulties in this

[5]Ralph Munn, *op. cit.*, p.37.

approach, since not much provision is made in library schools for this sort of recruit. The slower and more difficult alternative, reading and observation, supplemented by consultation with experienced librarians, is, however, not impossible. One who has had a very considerable advanced training and experience should be able to acquire a competent knowledge of a subject of not too great complexity, if the literature is available, without the necessity of enrolling in a course.

The danger in connection with securing a college librarian from the ranks of the teaching profession is not, in reality, the problem of technical skills so much as that of the personal qualifications necessary. It is obvious that this is not the place for the broken down or ineffective teacher. The good teacher on the other hand is not likely to be attracted by the present status and emoluments of the position.

There are two types of faculty members to whom the library might appeal and who would be able to do excellent work in the position. One is the individual who does not enjoy lecturing, and who is more interested in the bibliographic side of his subject and in individual conferences with students than in the formal presentation of his field. Such a man might be happier and more useful in the library than in routine class work. The second type is that of the faculty member to whom administrative work particularly appeals and who finds his greatest interest in the general problems and objectives of the campus. There are many members of faculties who will never be fully happy as reflective scholars, who like to deal with the concrete and practical problems of higher education, individuals who might be considered in connection with appointment of a dean or other administrative officer. The library, dealing as it does, with the problem of education as a whole and requiring administrative and financial skills, offers such indi-

viduals a real opportunity. There should be more re-
cruits from this source. Nothing could be more salu-
tary for the academic library profession than an
increase in the number of individuals crossing the
line which has heretofore divided college teachers and
college librarians.

This brings one to the third obligation of the college president mentioned above if he would secure
the most effective library service, namely, to raise the
librarian's status above what it is in most colleges.
There are several obvious reasons for this. The first
is that unless this is done it will be quite impossible
to secure men and women of the caliber desired for
this service. Few college professors, for example, who
might be attracted to the work of the library would
be willing to exchange their professional salary, their
secure tenure, their opportunity for sabbatical leave,
and their generally superior social status for a position
that usually offers less of a return in all of these respects. The fact that many librarians have not warranted a position comparable with that of faculty
members is beside the point, if one is interested in
securing a librarian who will.

There is a still more fundamental reason for improving the usual status of the librarian as compared
with that of his faculty colleagues. As colleges get
larger the tendency of the different elements to lose
contact with each other and to function as independent units is constantly to be combatted. The library,
it has already been noted, has been particularly liable
to this error, because of the difference of training and
viewpoint between the members of its staff and those
of the faculty. These differences are to be overcome
rather than emphasized. This calls for an organizational set-up which relates the librarian to the faculty
as closely as possible.

The writer knows of no study which has been made
on a national scale of the status of college librarians

in relation to that of their teaching colleagues. Mr.
C. G. Davidson has, however, investigated the subject
in 106 southern liberal arts colleges.[6] Replies to a
questionnaire concerning their rank, training and
other data were received from the librarians of all
but 24 of these, the ones not replying being presumably those with the poorer qualifications. Of those
reporting, 88 per cent were women, and 12 per cent
men, a fact which is significant only because the
women tended to have less training and a weaker
position than the men. In more than a fourth of the
colleges reporting the librarians were not members of
the faculty. In only 18 per cent of the colleges the
librarian had the rank of a professor, though to this
must be added 24 per cent in which the status was
the somewhat indeterminate one of "administrative
officer." These two rankings combined amount to 42
per cent of the colleges. In only 19 per cent of the
colleges did the librarian receive the salary of a professor. Only 66 per cent were eligible for membership
in the usual faculty club. It is quite evident that in
most of these colleges, if it is desired to integrate the
work of the library and that of the teaching staff, the
respective college presidents have a good deal to do.

What is involved, however, is something more than
merely a formal listing in the catalog. The objective
desired is a contact or association which will result in
natural discussion and a common understanding of
mutual problems. The personality, educational interest, and scholarly outlook of the librarian will have,
as already insisted, more to do with getting this done
than any other factor. But there are administrative
ways in which the matter can be facilitated. It seems
evident that the librarian should be a member of the

[6] "The Status of Librarians in Southern Liberal Arts Colleges"
(Unpublished Master's thesis, Graduate Library School, University of
Chicago). The A.L.A. *Survey of Libraries in the United States* (Chicago: A.L.A., 1926), I, chap. iv, contains considerable related data, but
does not cover the point in question.

faculty, if any educational responsibility is expected of him. It is not the title "professor" that is important, but his membership in the body which discusses and determines matters of the curriculum. There are certain committees of the faculty on which the librarian might serve, both for his contribution and for the increased effectiveness of the library's service which would result. In a number of institutions in which the curriculum is organized by divisions the librarian is made a member of one or more of these. At Swarthmore, for example, he is regularly invited to attend the social science divisional meetings. Departments should be encouraged to invite the librarian to be present when the work of large classes involving much library work is to be planned or new courses projected. All class syllabi and reading schedules should be subject to the criticism of the librarian from the standpoint of adequacy of materials available and the arrangements for their use.

These details deal with the librarian's relationship to the instructional staff. Some of these may not be universally applicable or desirable, but a wise administrator will find his own way of opening the doors of communication, understanding and mutual appreciation which too often have been closed. In addition to these matters, some of which are only suggestive in character, there are two important matters which affect the standing of the librarian. About one of them the president can probably do something; as regards the other, it is more doubtful.

The first of these is the librarian's standing in the library itself. Investigations on this point are very surprising. In the study of the libraries of southern liberal arts colleges cited above the following interesting data was revealed. In only 18 per cent of the colleges was the librarian responsible for the allocation of book funds, in 55 per cent for the decision on whether or not to accept gifts to the library, in 35 per cent for the selection of student assistants to work in the library, in 41 per cent for library hours, in 68 per cent for the rules for the circulation of books, in seven per cent for the final decision in the purchase of circulation books, in 57 per cent for the decision on the purchase of reference books, and in 57 per cent for the purchase of recreational books. It is evident that the administration of the library in such cases is really being carried by some outside force, usually a faculty library committee.

The relationship of the faculty library committee and the librarian in connection with book selection and the allocation of book funds will be discussed in some detail in a later chapter devoted to that subject. If the reader will permit the postponement of this phase of the question for the moment, the proper function of the library committee seems clear enough. Irked by too much interference some librarians have tended to deprecate the existence of such committees, and the writer has heard boasts in professional library meetings that "in my institution the library committee never meets." The librarian who cuts himself off from the aid which such a committee can render him is very foolish indeed. He needs the committee for advice and counsel on academic matters, and as an avenue through which criticisms of the library and suggestions for its improvement can be brought to his attention in a natural and unprovocative manner. The functions of such a committee, however, are advisory and informative, not administrative or executive. Administration by a faculty committee is sure to be slow, is likely to be vacillating and in the last analysis is lacking in responsibility. Experience has shown repeatedly that the only satisfactory way to administer the library is to put the authority in the hands of the librarian, set up for him contacts with the faculty which will be at the same time natural and official, and then to hold him responsible for its satisfactory administration. Special situations may call for other arrangements, but these should be recognized as special and temporary adjustments rather than the normal form of organization.

The other factor referred to is probably as important as any of those mentioned in opening doors of communication between the librarian and the teaching staff, but college presidents can do very little about it. That is the librarian's social standing and qualities. Informal contacts and natural friendships are of more value than official connections. The librarian's task of working with all members of the faculty makes the qualities which underlie successful social relationships of direct importance, and this should be kept in mind in making the appointment. Once made, administrative assistance is confined for the most part to providing a salary that will enable the librarian and his family to take part on equal terms in the social life of the community, and in opening doors to membership in the social organizations of the campus.

Should the librarian also teach? On this point there is a definite division of belief and practice. In most institutions the librarian does not do regular teaching work, very possibly because many of them have not been adequately qualified for it. More recently with better paid librarians, one finds a number of them taking part in the work of instruction as well. Thus the librarian of Pomona College is a regular member of the department of political science; the librarian of Fisk University, until his election to another post, an instructor in the department of philosophy; the librarian of Williams College, a member of the department of political science. The arguments advanced in favor of this practice are that (a) by becoming a member of a department the librarian bridges in his own person the "gap" which has been talked about, and sees the problems of the library from both points of view; (b) that he secures thereby standing on the campus that he would not have otherwise; and (c) that by this means far better qualified librarians can be secured for college work than would be possible otherwise for financial reasons.

Over against these arguments are several considerations. The library in most institutions is capable of absorbing all the attention and energy which one has at his disposal. A divided allegiance, furthermore, is difficult to maintain. Certainly the question of standing is to be settled by recognizing the importance of the librarian's work, rather than by decking him out in professorial bunting. The problem is one which probably does not admit of any uniform solution. One may say that where the duties of the library permit, some teaching may be a useful and helpful experience, particularly if it utilizes and keeps alive some special intellectual interest.

But care must be taken that this teaching is not at the expense of the library service to the institution as a whole, and that a potentially excellent librarian does not dissipate his interests and energies. Occasional teaching or that which is clearly subordinate to the librarian's principal job would seem to be all to the good, while to load the librarian down with large introductory classes would certainly be undesirable. Questions concerning courses in bibliography and in the use of the library are postponed for later discussion.

This chapter may conclude by drawing attention to a conception of the librarian's job which is unique in American college work and which has been fruitful in its results. In 1931 President Wood of Stephens College appointed Mr. B. Lamar Johnson librarian and dean of instruction. The conception back of this appointment was that the library contains the tools with which virtually all instruction must deal, and that the direction of the teaching program and the administration of the library was one, not two, jobs. This point of view regarded the library simply as the extension of the classroom. The beneficial results, so far as the circulation of library books is concerned, which followed this appointment have already been indicated. Whether such an arrangement would be equally satisfactory in institutions of a different character, the writer would not attempt to say. The conception back of this original and demonstrably fruitful idea, however, challenges the complacency with which many colleges regard their traditional organization and practice, namely, that the use of books is not an incidental aspect of instruction, but central and primary, and that library and classroom must therefore work as a single unit. It may not be wise in other situations to place the librarian in charge of instruction, but college administrators who turn from this solution will find it incumbent upon themselves to seek by other means the integration of effort which this solution achieved.

CHAPTER SIX

Making Books Accessible

WITH EVERYTHING WHICH HAS BEEN SAID AS TO THE DE-
sirability of a library administration closely integrated with teaching efforts, everyone will be in hearty
agreement. As soon as one attempts to define in specific terms what this seems to involve, difficulties or
disagreements immediately begin. These disagreements are due to two causes. In part they arise from
real differences of judgment as to the elements which
are most important and should be determinative in
that balancing of gains and losses which practical de-
cisions usually involve. In part, however, they are due
to confusions or misunderstandings. Librarians whose
underlying point of view is in thorough accord may
differ warmly on the desirability of some library practice because they are speaking with different situations in mind. Without therefore any claim or impli-
cation of a superior skill in such matters, a discussion
of these controversial issues seems warranted. On the
one hand, one may hope by the attention which has
been called to the centrality of the library in the work
of college instruction to tip the balance in some cases
in the choice of educational over against administrative ends. In the second place, it is possible that a
further discussion of library practice from the standpoint of student use may clarify somewhat the variations of practice in different types of institutions
which are often so confusing.

I plunge, therefore, *in medias res*. One of the most
controversial issues has been that of the open shelf

versus the closed shelf form of book administration. On this point there usually exists a tug of war between the faculty and the library staff. The educational principle here seems clear enough, to provide direct access of students to books. There are, of course, practical limits to this principle, such as a cost which the institution does not feel that it can afford, or the creation of conditions which definitely interfere with student use. We shall return to certain of these practical problems later. College libraries, however, do not seem to have been very clear on the general principle, but repeatedly have adopted unnecessarily measures which have separated students from books. This practice, on the face of it, is so obviously contrary to the purpose for which the books were bought as to require some explanation.

The original and no doubt the strongest factor has been the influence of what has been called the "rare book tradition." In the Middle Ages when books were copied by hand and were excessively rare, a library was something to be guarded with all possible care. Many of the earliest university book collections were chain libraries, *i.e.,* the books were chained to the desks or racks on which they had to be used. A number of the college libraries of Oxford and Cambridge have been found to have been originally of this character. In such circumstances there was bred an instinctive feeling which still influences us, that books must be exposed to no risks. Modern libraries are still enormously valuable, due to the great number of volumes they contain, but once the few rare or especially expensive ones are withdrawn for special handling, the individual items themselves are not so. Dr. Jessup, in one of his essays, draws an interesting comparison between the handling given books and that given scientific equipment and material. The latter, having come into the institution at a later period, enjoy a decidedly different status.

The typical chemistry building overflows with material: it fills the room and spills out into the corridors; its fumes rise to the heavens. It is true that there are chemical storehouses, but chemistry storage is a custodial job dealing with consumable material. . . . No one would expect the departments of chemistry, biology, botany and physics to house their material in some separate building, difficult of access, even though it were elaborately inventoried, efficiently managed and built of marble.[1]

This "rare book tradition" was a strong influence in the early American college libraries. They guarded their book treasures with great diligence, many of them keeping them on shelves under lock and key. A rule of the Brown University Library in its earliest days was no doubt an extreme case, but illustrates the point of view: "Students shall come to the library four at a time when sent for by the librarian, and they shall not enter the library beyond the table of the librarian on penalty of 3d. for every offense."[2] The continuity of such practices with the older chained book libraries is obvious, and their relation to the modern closed shelf practice which forbids passage of students beyond the delivery desk is plain enough. From about 1880 on, the trend was toward freer access, but the different status of current books since their production by the tens of thousands per year has never been fully accepted.

A second factor in this country has been the influence of the great research libraries. It is curious that the first graduate schools with their emphasis on first hand investigation were definite influences toward greater accessibility of books and freedom in their use. This greater freedom, however, as the institutions developed, tended to become restricted to graduate stu-

[1]Memorandum in Ralph Munn, *Conditions and Trends in Education for Librarianship* (New York: The Carnegie Corporation, 1936), p.42.
[2]Cited in Lodilla Ambrose, "A Study of College Libraries," *Library Journal*, XVIII (April, 1893), 114.

dents, who were admitted freely to the stacks, given desks within arm's reach of their material and otherwise aided. The increasingly large bodies of undergraduate students were gradually excluded. The prestige of these great libraries, plus the ability of their librarians, made them the models and leaders in matters of library administration. Smaller institutions have felt quite secure and efficient so long as they were sure that they were following the practices of such libraries as those of Harvard, Michigan or Columbia. The differences in the problems to be met too often have been overlooked in the satisfaction of being in such good company.

To these two factors must be attributed a good deal of the willingness of college communities to keep the book collection closed off from direct student use. They do not, of course, cover all of the facts. Many libraries have adopted this method of administration because of their actual experience of book losses and other undesirable results in connection with free admission to their stacks. This applies particularly to those universities with student enrolments in the thousands and with large book collections to be preserved and administered. These libraries constitute, however, a special group with special problems not characteristic of colleges in general. Before discussing their particular problems, it is necessary to raise the basic question: Is it really desirable or important for college students to have direct access to the book collection of their college libraries? This is by no means a rhetorical question. There is a strong feeling among many librarians that "seeing the backs of the books does not of itself bring about reading," that it is not really important to admit students to free use of the shelves, and that therefore the undoubted factor of greater ease of library administration on the closed shelf basis should be decisive. While the writer of this report would admit that there are other more important factors in determining the amount of reading, it is believed that direct access to books helps, and is a contribution which the library staff can make toward that desired end.

The first reason why direct access to the book stacks is desirable is the obvious fact that if the student cannot examine the shelves, he must know in advance the book he wants to read. Not only must he have a general knowledge of the book, he must have a sufficiently exact knowledge of the author or the title to locate it on a card. The difficulty can be stated more clearly by an illustration. Suppose a student wants to read the recent volume, *Germany Enters the Third Reich.* In a library of fair size it is almost hopeless—or at least discouraging—to look for the book by its title, since there will probably be from several score to several hundreds of cards bearing the key word, *Germany.* To locate the book with any celerity, it is necessary that the student know the name of the author. If he recalls that it is Hoover and looks for this name in the catalog, he will find a great many cards, but most of these will be for books by or about one Herbert Hoover, recent president of the United States and titular leader of the Republican party. If persistent enough, the student can by going through all the author cards by that name discover that the book desired was by Calvin B. Hoover and can then fill out the call slip and request the book. Unless, however, the desire for the book was strong, the chances are that the student will drop the matter after his first repulse at the catalog. The same fundamental problem can be illustrated from the standpoint of the title. A student has heard a good deal, let us say, about E. A. Robinson and has decided that he would like to read some of his verse. In the card catalog he finds a number of titles, concerning none of which he has any knowledge. He chooses blindly *Tristram,* only to find when the volume comes out of the mill that it is a single poem of

210 pages which must be read in its entirety to be appreciated. An actual case can be cited in which a student wanted to read something by Karl Marx. He looked in the card catalog and requested the volume *Capital,* only to find it a tedious work of more than 500 pages which he returned almost immediately. Had he been able to look at the books themselves he probably would have chosen *The Communist Manifesto,* which he might have actually read. Probably a more frequent case is that which arises when an undergraduate wants to read something on the Middle Ages, or on some general field of interest such as astronomy. Even though titles on the topic may be listed in the catalog, there is no indication which of the books are suitable for introductory reading. The basic difficulty in all of these cases is of course that the student does not know what he wants, and no catalog can be built which will give an answer to a question which can be stated only in vague or very general terms. Yet such vague and tentative gropings are the tender shoots of mental growth which should receive the most careful nurture.

What the closed shelf system does is thus to interpose between the student and his reading the necessity of a definite and exact knowledge of the book which is wanted. To return to the first illustration used above, if the student had looked in the catalog for the volume by Calvin Bryce Hoover, *Germany Enters the Third Reich,* he would have encountered no difficulty. But this necessity of knowing the author's name and initials or the exact title, means that the system tends to discourage all except assigned reading, that is, reading in which this bibliographical knowledge has been supplied by the instructor. The librarian whose training has emphasized both correct bibliographical data and the organization of the catalog perhaps does not sense this psychological barrier.

Indeed it can be strongly argued and ought to be

carefully considered whether current American library practice has not reversed the methods which should be used in service to graduates and undergraduates respectively. Admission to the stacks is commonly granted to graduate students and faculty members, and is commonly denied in the large universities and in perhaps half the colleges to undergraduates. But the graduate student is pursuing a specialized problem, with the general literature and major sources of which he is acquainted, and which he investigates largely by following up citations encountered in his reading. In other words, he has at his command the bibliographical knowledge referred to above which enables him to use the catalog and get at the material desired. The undergraduate on the other hand has a wider and far less precise interest, and usually has little knowledge of the various bibliographic guides which are available.

European libraries offer an interesting contrast in this respect to the American practice. The great research libraries rarely admit readers to their stacks; yet these are maintained only for advanced students and trained scholars. For introductory study small open shelf libraries are usually maintained. In Oxford those open shelf collections are in the residential colleges. In Germany they are the seminar libraries or institute libraries. We reverse this process, admitting the graduate but excluding the undergraduate student. It seems plain that this generally accepted procedure is a product of the American class system of instruction, and is predicated on the theory that virtually all undergraduate reading will be of specific assignments. There are abundant signs that this sort of college teaching is being modified at least in part, and library practice must reexamine its procedures with this in mind.

There are other advantages in providing direct access to books besides escaping the demand for exact bibliographical knowledge which the catalog makes of a would-be reader. One is the avoidance of the necessity of standing in line and waiting one's turn at the service desk which the closed shelf system requires. The voluntary testimony of a reader written to express appreciation for a change from a closed to an open stack system offers perhaps the best exposition of this practical point:

You were not infrequently told after you had waited from five to fifteen minutes that all copies of the book were in use; so you meekly requested another title on your list and waited again. After spending considerable time in obtaining a book, you might find it contained a reference so brief that you could read it in half the time required to get it. After going through this routine day after day and week after week, it was likely to have a cumulatingly irritating effect. . . . This irritation may have been senseless; however, it was likely to develop into a feeling of frustration, ending in one of intense antagonism for the assistants, who probably were doing their best to give you what you wanted.

This description of the state of exasperation induced by the functioning of the closed shelf system is taken from a student's letter commenting on the change to an open shelf system in Teachers College, Columbia.[3] The difficulty here is perhaps primarily psychological, but it is no less real for that reason. The actual time spent is not great, since most libraries are now quite efficient in desk delivery service. But there is nothing more disagreeable than filling out forms and standing in line. Even if one spent as much time in the process of getting the book oneself, which is quite likely, there is still a difference. The time is spent actively in looking for the book, rather than in waiting. Furthermore, in looking on the shelf itself rather than in a catalog, other volumes on the subject are noted and something

[3]Quoted in A. L. Hill, "Reserve Books on Open Shelves," *Wilson Bulletin,* V, 621f.

equally as satisfactory perhaps chosen if the sought for item is out.[4]

Most readers, however, will feel that the major reason for the open shelf practice remains to be stated. It is that books on locked or closed shelves are dumb and meaningless—so many physical objects to be stored and kept in order. Displayed to possible readers, the collection becomes alive with suggestion and allure. The problem of education is to a large extent one of creating an environment which is intellectually stimulating. The library is a cultural and educational influence of great potential power. To remove the books from sight is a step to be deplored on educational and moral grounds. Long ago Plato remarked that the "pursuit of wisdom is not, as fools suppose, crabbed and dull, but as musical as Apollo's lyre," but not all undergraduates have made this discovery. There probably is no better way to bring about this discovery, which each one must make for himself, than by displaying in their infinite variety the volumes which the college has chosen for its book collection. Colleges are not merely examining or graduating boards, but opportunities for growth and self development under as nearly ideal conditions as can be created for the crucial years between youth and adulthood. Such ideal conditions can scarcely be said to exist where students are not conscious of the presence of books.

The above remarks are addressed to the educational desirability of direct access to books, a postulate which provides, if granted, the point of departure for college library practice. They do not deal with the limits within which this access is practicable, nor with the special problems of the large universities, particularly

[4]The point which is made can be easily verified. Practically all colleges and universities grant stack permits to faculty members. Except in the very large libraries, the majority of faculty members prefer to get their own books rather than have the attendant fetch the volume, though this usually means climbing steps. Certainly this is true of those who use the library regularly.

those located in a metropolitan area, with student enrolments running into many thousands. The libraries of these institutions have found it necessary to prohibit direct entry into the book stacks to students and the general public. When thousands of readers are to be served, it is impossible for them to be known by face or instructed in the arrangements of a large stack. Open stacks in such conditions involve a risk which few libraries would want to take, as well as a disruption and impairment of service which would be objectionable to all concerned. The facts have never been better stated than by Dr. Bishop at the time of the planning of the University of Michigan Library:

To my mind there is no more vital force in the education of students than intimate and immediate personal contact with the whole of the university library. In my own case, I feel that the privilege of admission to the stacks which was given me in my last two years as a student here did more to produce a scholarly attitude toward my work than any other single advantage offered by the University. . . . It seems to me that one of the chief aims of university education is to make the student familiar with the literature of the great subjects of instruction and to teach him to make his own judgments on the literature.

There are, however, extremely practical difficulties in the way of free admission for the whole student body to the entire contents of the book stacks of any modern library. These difficulties are so real that I found myself unable to plan a new library building for the University of Michigan as to solve them. They are partly structural, partly financial, partly administrative. I need not enumerate them. . . . Anyone who can plan a library building to house half a million or more volumes for an institution of six to ten thousand students and arrange to have unlimited free access to the book shelves for the entire student body or even the greater part of it, will produce an advance in library science and higher education incomparably greater than anything which has been done up to the present time. I confess that the problem is beyond me except by the use of practically unlimited funds for building and administration.[5]

In this statement written some years ago Dr. Bishop poses the problem of these large university libraries. The practical necessity of the closed stacks does not in the least modify its undesirability from an educational standpoint. This has become even clearer since he wrote this statement. The result of the dilemma has been that an increasing number of leading universities in which the book stacks are closed to undergraduates have felt it necessary in recent years to provide other means by which these students may have direct access to a considerable number of books.

The arrangements made for undergraduate readers by Columbia University at the time of the erection of South Hall, the university library, while admittedly not ideal, illustrate this conviction. Since there was no difference of opinion as to the necessity of closed stacks for the general collection, special quarters were provided for the work of the undergraduates of the college. These consist of six rooms: an open shelf reading room containing about 15,000 selected volumes; a special open shelf college reference room; a periodical, current literature, and science reading room; a working office for the college library staff; stack space with a delivery desk for a large reserved book collection; and a sixth room now used for student conferences and committee meetings. The books in this section, though listed in the union catalog, belong primarily and permanently to the "College Study," as it is called. The College Study is supplemented by the University Browsing Room and the several divisional reading rooms in which undergraduates have, along with graduate and other readers, direct access to special book collections.

[5]Quoted in Strong, "Student Access to Book Collections," *Library Journal,* XLIV (1919), 439.

Similar provisions have been provided or are being planned by other institutions, though no common form has as yet developed. The University of Chicago in connection with its new plan of study felt it essential to provide a special "college" library. This library is housed in one of the instructional halls. Consultation offices for certain of the basic college courses are at each end of the reading room. It is true that the open shelf arrangements, as in the Columbia College Study, are confined chiefly to the optional readings and reference tools. There is however no elaborate catalog to be consulted, the syllabi of the various courses being the guide to the materials housed. This library cannot be understood apart from a knowledge of the "College Plan" of the University of Chicago which it was devised to serve, and also certain local factors, one of the most important being the large number of day students in the college. Its keynotes are simplicity of arrangements, limitation of titles to those involved in the new courses of study, multiplicity of copies of those titles, and a willingness of the staff to modify regulations constantly in the light of the changing factors of demand and supply as regards the books. This library was preceded in time and strongly influenced by the open shelf library of the Modern Language Division housed in the same building. Both are supplemented by open shelf libraries of considerable extent located in residence halls, and, for students in the upper division, by the numerous departmental libraries of the University. Plans for library development at Chicago call for a special building for and considerable expansion of the College Library.

In Harvard and Yale the educational value of providing undergraduates with direct access to books has been recognized and given even more adequate expression. Harvard has had for some years a number of open shelf special libraries for undergraduate use. In addition to the open reserves in the general reading room in Widener Memorial Library, there are a freshman library of perhaps five thousand volumes, a collection on economics, politics and government, and other special collections for undergraduate use. Open shelf libraries of approximately ten thousand volumes each have recently been established in each of the residential Houses. These libraries will be discussed in some detail in the next chapter. The arrangements at Yale are similar. Much undergraduate reading and study is done in the open-shelf collection in the Linonia and Brothers Library. Libraries similar in character to this collection have been set up in nine residential college units.

In the University of Minnesota a special library has been provided on the insistence of the faculty for the students of the General College. The library is located in the building used for this special educational undertaking and its arrangements are determined by the faculty in charge of this college.

There are many other open shelf collections in large university libraries which could be cited, but most of these on examination prove to be special collections of one sort or another, or open shelf reserve book collections which will be treated later, rather than conscious efforts to solve the library problem for undergraduates. The developments cited are evidences of the growing realization that a large book collection approached by means of a card catalog containing millions of cards, for all its value for research, fails to contribute as fully as books should to the life of college students. In the light of these endeavors of some of the larger libraries, to overcome the handicap of their size and to provide easy access to books for their undergraduates, the closed shelf practices of smaller libraries would seem to be a gratuitous sacrifice of the one advantage which these libraries possess.

This recognition by college administrators of the

impotence of closed book collections to interest students in books has found expression in another direction. Combining with an aesthetic reaction against the dark and uninviting manner in which the books are displayed in most library stacks, many libraries have adopted the arrangement known as a "browsing room." These rooms vary considerably in details, but are usually open shelf collections containing the more generally recognized English classics and other volumes selected for their cultural value but not for curricular purposes. In scope and size they range all the way from such collections as that of the Linonia and Brothers Room at Yale, which is a well rounded collection of about 17,000 volumes, virtually an open shelf college library in itself, to a few hundred volumes of belles-lettres encased in fine bindings. The rooms are usually more expensively decorated than the rest of the library and more comfortably furnished. The idea has appealed to friends and alumni, and many of these rooms are endowed. Regulations vary. In many of them studying, evidenced by note taking, is forbidden. Some permit the books to circulate, others require them to be used in the room. The writer has during the year visited a number of these "browsing rooms." In the large university centers these rooms seem as a general rule to be well used. The attendance must be considered, however, in the light of the thousands of readers in these communities —students, instructors, extension and part-time students, and the families of those whose work is in the university, as well as of the fact that it is usually the only general reading collection which is easily accessible. In these large centers each browsing room must be judged with reference to the other facilities of the library and the particular service it is attempting to contribute.

In the smaller academic centers the general rule seems to be that the browsing rooms have a small, though usually fairly constant, clientele. Several institutions could be cited in which the librarians were disturbed over the failure of the students to make use of these magnificently equipped rooms. In more than one no readers were found in the browsing room on the days on which they were visited. In one institution the librarian was endeavoring to vitalize the room by placing in it groups of books made up for certain student organizations, such as the Foreign Affairs Club and the Liberal Club. In another the room contained a number of the more popular current magazines.

No one who believes in libraries at all could raise objections to a browsing room as such. To provide a beautiful room and comfortable chairs and a collection of books worth reading is in itself a very useful thing to do. Such collections increase in value in proportion to the lack of these qualities of comfort and accessibility in the rest of the library. If the books contained in it range over the undergraduate curriculum, it becomes a miniature open shelf library such as has been argued for above. Most browsing rooms, however, avoid on principle books relating to the curriculum, offering to their readers either literary classics or the better current publications of general interest or a combination of the two. The objective is usually said to be recreational and cultural.

It seems obvious that these rooms are in large part a reaction against the form our libraries have taken in the last few decades, or stated more kindly, an effort to supply in a different form the lost literary stimulus which the small college library offered a generation ago. One cannot pass judgment on them in a group. In many situations, they render no doubt a very desirable and valuable service. But two questions concerning them have to be raised. The first is whether they do not apply the best resources of the library to what is a useful but nevertheless a definitely secondary function of the institution, namely, recreational and other non-curricular reading. It does seem somewhat absurd for a college to employ a staff of specialists who plan the courses of reading and study which are believed to be most rewarding for undergraduate pursuit, and then to provide in its library special inducements of various sorts for the non-curricular reading. The procedure seems to imply a lack of confidence in the curriculum, a belief, that is, that the most important reading is left out of the course of study. If so, it would seem that a revision of the curriculum would be in order. One can scarcely resist the impression that in this development two influences have been at work. One is that librarians as a group have stood outside the major instructional program and, naturally enough, have developed a special interest in the non-curricular reading of students. This field has been their special province and they have been quick to see in this area the value of principles which are equally applicable to the whole program of the library. The second is that college presidents have found in the browsing room arrangement both compensation for the reservations and complexities which have developed elsewhere, and also a clear provision for undergraduate self-education through books. The difficulty with the latter point is not that it is untrue, but rather that the college has declared by every means at its disposal its conviction that this education for most students is to be more satisfactorily secured by the study of other subjects and a different set of books from those which the browsing room offers.

The second question is simply whether the browsing room works, whether, that is, it accomplishes with a sufficient number of undergraduates its task of interesting them in the literature which it puts on its shelves. The results vary of course. A great deal appears to depend on whether the room is easily accessible, a good deal on the freshness and interest of the book collection, and a good deal on the skill of the library staff in popularizing the room. The typical oak paneled room in the college library with fine editions of the classics does not seem in fact to have many readers. This is not surprising, for after all the chief business of college students is reading, and recreation on a college campus is likely to take other forms. One very competent librarian summed up the situation in his library with the statement that six or eight students a year "got an education out of the room," and on this ground it could be justified. Whether this represents the optimum investment of the funds involved, the college itself must decide.

Without therefore having anything but praise for the browsing room itself, one may conclude that it has for most colleges been a too easy substitute for a much more thorough program of making books available and attractive, and that to derive the fullest benefit from it, it should in most situations be related more definitely to some aspect of the curricular program.

Up to the present nothing has been said of that important collection, books placed on reserve. The figures cited earlier in this volume indicate that from 50 to 90 per cent of the student book withdrawals in most college libraries are from this group of books. For a large portion of the student body the reserved book room is the college library.

The unsatisfactoriness of the reserved book arrangements in most colleges is agreed to by students, librarians and instructors alike. The brief periods for which the books may be used, the necessity for many duplicates, the waste involved when reading lists are changed, the large number of volumes tied up which are not used, the crowded, noisy and restless condition of the reserved book reading room, and the tendency of students never to go beyond the books given this special handling, are all causes of complaint.

The original purpose of the usual reserved book arrangements is clear enough. The system of class reading assignments meant that the same pages had to be read at the same time by all members of the class. Some mechanism had to be devised, therefore, to increase the mobility or serviceableness of each book during the period of general demand for it. That faculty members are trying to use the reserved book room in many libraries for purposes other than this simple original purpose seems easily demonstrable. "The tendencies observable in this part of the library are of more than passing interest." Before going on with the discussion, a few illustrations of what occurs in the average reserved book room may be cited.

In Oregon State College, Miss Constance Beall examined the records of the books on reserve for the fall semester of 1937. The statistics compiled revealed that 48 per cent of the books had not been used.

A study at Princeton covering the spring semester in 1934 showed that of 4,224 volumes on reserve, 47.4 per cent were used less than eight times. Since nine readers could withdraw a book for two weeks each during a semester, it would appear that this percentage for the most part did not belong on reserve.

A study at the University of Nebraska made by Professor Worcester of the Teachers College showed that "only 25 per cent of the books placed on reserve were used by students enough to justify their being placed there." The actual figures were as follows: 6,181 volumes were on reserve; 4,594 or 74 per cent were used less than nine times; 1,987 or 32 per cent were not used at all. One instructor placed 455 volumes on reserve, 149 not being used at all, and only 3 being used more than 6 times.

In the University of Texas, of 7,060 volumes on reserve during the year 1936-37, 2,133 or 32 per cent were not used.[6]

*The data in this and the two previous cases are taken from the valuable memorandum of Mr. T. W. Koch of Northwestern University Library, "Further Light on the Reserve Book Problem" (Mimeo.; Evanston, Ill., 1937). The memorandum was privately distributed by the author.

In the University of Minnesota a study of the reserved book collection in 1934 by Miss Helen Smith of the library staff revealed that 5,989 titles (20,312 volumes) were placed on reserve, that 3,353 (56 per cent) titles were used 9 times or less, and that 1,169 titles were not used at all.

Such figures as these seem to be characteristic, except perhaps in some of the smaller libraries. They are due in part of course to carelessness and inertia on the part of faculty members in leaving on their reserved book lists titles which are no longer used in the course. But they are not due solely to this cause. Of this the study by Miss Smith of the University of Minnesota Library offers a statistical demonstration. The facts of nonuse in considerable detail were sent to all faculty members concerned, and a revision of reserved lists requested. The faculty attitude toward this communication was appreciative, and in the following semester the number of books on reserve was reduced by 1,267 volumes. This, however, was only 6 per cent of the 20,312 volumes reserved the previous term, which would seem to represent about the margin of obvious carelessness and error. It is plain that other factors are at work. One, of course, is an admirable faculty optimism as to the amount of reading that a class will do, which causes books to be put on reserve to take care of the hoped-for rush. It is only necessary to call attention to the figures of actual use to correct these errors of judgment. Instructors who place from one to two hundred books on reserve, however, do not really expect all these books to be used heavily. Why then do they put them there? Inquiry points to the conclusion that they are trying to get them out of the stacks with the thought that individual books are more or less buried when left in the stacks, and that the greater accessibility secured may result in some of the titles being used which otherwise would have remained untouched. Faculty members have quite generally fallen into the habit of placing on reserve all the books pertaining to a course given, irrespective of whether or not they will be in heavy demand. Instructors and librarians in other words are working at cross purposes in the reserved book room to a considerable extent. The former are endeavoring, rather vaguely, to make of it a more easily accessible college library; the latter merely to increase the circulation of books under heavy demand.

If this analysis is correct, it will not solve the problem merely to urge instructors to revise their reading lists. This will no doubt reduce the reserves to some extent and will free some books for general use which should not be tied up. Nor will it solve the underlying problem to point out to instructors that they are defeating their own ends by placing books which will be used only a few times under the strict regulations of the reserved collection. The instructor has the right to ask of the librarian, "Well, what is the answer? Can you devise some plan by which my students may come into contact with the books I want them to know and read?" It is plain that this brings us back to the same problem which has been considered, and reinforces the argument which has been presented. A number of leading institutions were cited which have recognized the inadequacy of great research collections to provide library service appropriate to undergraduate needs, and have set up special collections for this purpose. We now see that even where this has not been recognized by the institution, internal developments have been moving in the same direction.

This discussion of the unsatisfactory reserved book arrangements in most libraries raises in more specific form than in the treatment above the question how direct access can be best provided. It is obvious that the extent to which the problem can be solved and the form of the solution will depend on a number of factors, the chief one being the size of the student body.

There is, first, the college in which the student body and book collection are of small or moderate proportions. The solution here would seem obvious, and it is probably the best of all plans so long as it is workable. It is to insist that the entire library is the student's workshop, and to throw all forces and influences toward its full use. If the program is wholeheartedly agreed to and carried out, faculty members may be led to place on reserve only those books which will be under pressure of use, others being left on the shelves. This will enable the recommended or optional books to be withdrawn freely by class members and to be utilized by other members of the academic community, and will also direct the students' attention to everything the library possesses on that subject. In libraries of this category the book collection is not so great as to confuse the student nor will the distance to the shelf be great. One must struggle here of course against the current type of stack construction, which lends little encouragement to book use. Local conditions will always have to be appraised in each instance. The general principle, however, of throwing the faculty and students back to the use of the main collection, except for those books which must go on reserve is surely sound.

In libraries of this category one can sometimes go a step further and abolish the reserved book room outright. Several institutions have shown that this is possible. The best illustration is the excellent and much used library of Vassar College.

The Vassar Library is administered on the principle of open reserves, the books so denominated being held in the building except for overnight use. The older part of the library was built on the alcove plan, each alcove opening on the main reading rooms. At the entrance to most alcoves is a low book case of two or three shelves, on which are placed the reserves for the class or classes using the material located on the

shelves of the alcove to its rear. In a new wing recently built the older alcove form is discarded for a
modern—not nearly so attractive but probably more
economical—book stack. In this wing the class reserves
are placed on shelves, usually in the corridors, as near
as possible to the main collection on each subject.
Books taken from the reserves for overnight use are
charged at the main desk near the entrance to the
library. The advantages of such a system are that the
reserves are located all over the building and diffuse
the noise and commotion which other systems concen-
trate in one room, that all material is open to free
access, and most important of all, reserve books on a
topic are never more than one or two steps from the
rest of the material which the library possesses on the
subject. Logically this system can be carried still further—the books on reserve could be so marked and
left in their usual place on the shelves. The Vassar
system does this to some extent, books so designated
being marked "Not to be taken from the Library."
The special reserve shelf, however, is preferred, since
it reduces the confusion caused by books being returned to the main shelves in the wrong place, and
eliminates difficulties otherwise encountered in keeping the books on the main shelves upright. It is obvious that a system of this sort can be modified, if
thought desirable, by holding at the central desk those
volumes under special pressure, a dummy or notice on
the reserved book shelf directing the reader to call for
the title there. In this effort to avoid an artificial separation between books placed on reserve and other
books on the topic the library staff is ably reinforced
by the Vassar instructional staff. The Department of
History, for example, issues a memorandum concerning its introductory courses which reads in part as
follows:

The Vassar College Library is the laboratory of the

student of history. As it affords the student what will be perhaps the only experience in her lifetime of free access to the shelves of a first class library, it is the custom of the Department of History not to reserve on special shelves books recommended for a course. Instead the student is encouraged to select for herself the books which she will read and study.[7]

Granting modifications of this plan to meet particular circumstances, the general principle of reducing reserves to those books which necessitate special control and utilizing the entire book collection seems the most desirable solution of the reserved book room problem for the smaller library. The solution is not necessarily limited to the small library. The new plans for the "humanistic laboratory" of Princeton University have been developed along these lines. The emphasis falls on opportunities and aids for the undergraduate to use the entire collection, not some selected group of books. But it must be associated with a program designed to make the general stack collection function as an active educational influence. This will certainly involve open stacks, easier physical access if possible, better lighting and guides for readers, and quite possibly the removal of dead wood from the book collection.

This solution is limited, however, to those situations in which the central book collection can be made an active working tool for undergraduate use. In those institutions where the student body is so large as to make this impossible, or where the book collection is too big for undergraduates to handle either from the standpoint of finding the books wanted or from the standpoint of the number of stack levels to be climbed, this solution is out of the question. Colleges in which this is the case constitute a second group. They seem shut up to the necessity of creating some

[7]Departmental memorandum, 12 November 1937 FB.

smaller collection of books selected and administered for undergraduate use. In this group fall the institutions cited earlier in this chapter. Also in it are many of the institutions in which the reserved book room has come to be recognized as virtually the undergraduate library. The blind development of the latter, which frequently contains from eight to fifteen thousand volumes representing the required reading and a large body of associated or recommended material, needs only to be recognized and critically guided.

In these "college" libraries, whether in the same building as the main book collection or in a separate structure, there is no debate concerning those volumes which will not be in heavy demand. All would agree to the desirability of open shelf arrangements and complete freedom of access for this material. Required readings, on the contrary, are in most cases held behind a desk and supplied on demand. Greater ease of access in their case means simply quick service and an ability to request the book by its title rather than by its call number. Few would deny the theoretic desirability of direct access to these books also and these arguments need not be repeated. Evidence that a considerable and apparently an increasing number of libraries have found a practical means of providing this remains to be presented.

The solution which as has been found to function very satisfactorily in a number of institutions is to place an attendant's desk at the door and to check all books being carried out of the room. Yale has had this system for its reserved book room for a number of years. In 1930 the Teachers College Library of Columbia University transferred the 13,000 volumes held on reserve to an open shelf basis, after experimenting for a year with a smaller collection. To these reserves have been added other materials. The social science reading room contains on open shelves the course reserves plus nearly all books published in this field since 1930 which the library has acquired. Although Teachers College serves some six thousand students, the change was greeted with elation by the students and no serious difficulties have yet been encountered.[8] In 1936 the Duke University Library broke away from its closed shelf reserved book system to open reserves with an attendant at the door. The change has been received with approval by both students and faculty. The University of Michigan has a similar plan of operation for its Basement Study Hall, chiefly used for the more advanced undergraduate courses. Harvard College has had for some years the several open shelf-reading rooms referred to above, most though not all of the material being directly available to the student. The statement of Mr. Koch in his memorandum referred to above may be quoted in summary of these developments: "Experience of the past two years indicates that the system of open shelves for reserved books is rapidly gaining favor among both faculty and students. Careful supervision of students at the exit of the Reserve Reading Room has practically ended loss of books from open shelves."[9] Where this method of handling reserved books is practical it is obvious that the separation of required and recommended books is no longer necessary. This distinction, always undesirable, will become increasingly meaningless as colleges work out more clearly means of adjusting teaching programs to the individual needs of students. A college study—to borrow Columbia's phrase—can thus be visualized which would supply the required course readings, related volumes on special topics, books to supplement individual deficiencies, some reference tools and some of those books for which browsing rooms are often constructed and maintained.

[8]See A. L. Hill, "Reserve Books on Open Shelves," *Wilson Bulletin*, V (June, 1931), 621 ff.
[9]T. W. Koch, *op. cit.*, p.2.

There is one danger in connection with such a plan for an open shelf library which needs to be kept in mind. It is that once selected it will become fixed and within a few years dead and uninteresting. Examples of such collections are not difficult to cite. The college library will need additions and also removals. This implies that the catalog provided in the room should be of the simplest sort, short title catalogs such as are provided in the Yale college libraries. Opinions differ as to whether entries for these books should appear in the main catalog. Chicago does not enter cards for books in the college library, but most institutions do so. If the latter policy is adopted, books permanently fixed in the college library should certainly be so marked—Shakespeare, the Bible and others. About others one cannot be so sure. There are three alternatives: to charge the material out to the college library through the circulation desk, to use the half card device which states that the next card refers to a book located in this collection, or to stamp the cards in the main catalog, crossing this out when the book is returned to the main collection.

It is probably unnecessary to add a protest against the too frequent assumption that all reserved books should be subject to the same rules. Although many of the volumes in this category will be limited to a two or three hour circulation, others may be allowed to circulate for three or five days.[10] It may also be mentioned that no matter how successful an open shelf reserved book arrangement may be, a few volumes will always occasion difficulty. In such cases, it is possible to transfer the troublesome material to the attendant's desk.

Such open shelf college libraries in institutions where the main book collection cannot be thrown widely open may have various modifications, accord-

[10]The University of Georgia Library, for example, has successfully made this distinction in closed shelf reserves, the Duke University Library in open shelf reserves.

ing to local needs and facilities. Where graduate reading rooms exist it may be felt desirable to throw a good deal of the junior-senior reading into those graduate rooms, particularly if the graduate school is small and there are several reading rooms developed to serve divisional interests. In such cases the college library would be developed and staffed to provide particularly for freshmen and sophomores. The justification for such a distinction would be the gradual extension of graduate school methods of instruction into the work of the junior-senior years, and the developing specialized interest of the advanced undergraduate student. Where the graduate school is large, however, and its special reading rooms crowded, the presence of undergraduates might be undesirable.

While such an arrangement as has been described has proven practical and useful in a number of institutions, it is not claimed that it should be adopted by all. Special circumstances and local conditions make it doubtless necessary in many cases to continue to handle assigned readings over a counter. The metropolitan universities in particular constitute a group to themselves so far as the problem of free access is concerned. Some of these have tried open shelf plans and abandoned them.[11] Every institution is to some extent a special case and must be a law unto itself. Its own experience will be regulatory; yet the facts entering into this experience need to be constantly criticized in the light of the results achieved elsewhere.

Perhaps a word may be added on one detail of reserved book room administration. Great numbers of duplicates are always an administrative problem. The plan followed at Amherst and elsewhere of operating

[11]The University of Chicago, for example, adopted the open shelf method of handling reserves in 1928-29. These reserves were gradually transferred back to the closed shelves, until in 1936-37 the open reserves in Harper Hall were entirely abandoned. In the meanwhile the College Library had been established, but it does not provide much free access to books. The University of California also experimented with and abandoned open shelf reserves.

a duplicate collection, quite separate from the general collection, has certain advantages. At Amherst the first two copies of all books purchased go into the general collection; all further copies belong to the duplicate collection, which when not in use is shelved separately in the library basement. When reading lists are changed, these duplicate copies are disposed of, rather than being added to the main collection. The arrangement has the advantages of keeping before the attention large quantities of textbook material which should be eliminated when their period of usefulness has ceased, greater expedition in getting such books ready for use, and certain conveniences of handling, particularly in avoiding the shifting and rearranging of books in the main stacks when the reserved material is withdrawn and replaced. This plan also has the advantage of holding in the general collection one or two copies of titles on reserve for the use of the general body of readers. Where funds do not permit the purchase of such extra copies and the usual system of transfer of books from the main collection to the reserved collection is followed, the half card device placed in front of the main entry card of titles transferred is a very great convenience to general readers. Care must be observed, however, to get this half card out when the book is returned to its permanent location. How far the library should go in the purchase of these duplicates will be considered below in the chapter on book selection.

The writer would like to chronicle the imminent demise of the reserve book system as we know it. The announcement, however, like that of Mark Twain's death, would be premature. Though some contraction in the amount of college reading handled in this way is to be observed in some institutions, the evidence is by no means uniform. Two tendencies in college teaching are to be observed. In some institutions one notes a tendency to designate topics or fields to be covered with indications of various books which might serve the purpose, and also an increase in the amount of special studies undertaken by the student under preceptorial or tutorial direction. This process results of course in fewer books on the reserved shelves. In other institutions a reconsideration of the objectives and materials of courses has resulted in a more definite list of "indispensable readings," and a demand rather for more adequate provision of these books by the college library or some other agency. Both trends are no doubt sound. With all recognition of individual differences of ability and preparation there will still remain many books which virtually all students in a course must use. We shall not get away from the problem of books wanted by a number of readers. Nevertheless the typical reserved book room should and can be changed in spirit and in form. Books which all the class must read can be supplied in many cases by other more effective means. It would probably be a kindness to most students and certainly an educational gain, if they were required to buy more of their indispensable books than they do in most colleges. The use of cheaper reprints and carefully planned rental sets are already being brought in to help solve the problem. On the other hand, modifications of college library architecture making the main collection more usable will reduce the congestion at the reserved book desk in many libraries. Through more careful planning of courses and closer cooperation between faculty and library staff, a three- or five-day period of use can be secured for a large number of the books related to the work of the class. Even without much change in teaching methods such procedures would greatly reduce the scope of the reserved collection and mitigate its evils.[12]

Throughout this chapter a plea has been made for

[12]A most helpful article on the administration of an open shelf reserved book room is R. F. Beach, "Some Useful Techniques in the Reserve Book Room," *A.L.A. Bulletin*, XXXIII (March, 1939), 185-87. The author describes the procedures followed in the Berea College Library.

direct access to the book shelves. A word is due on the two-fold subject of book thefts and book displacements which might result from such openness of access. Displacements of books are no doubt increased by admitting students to the stacks but this can be offset by increasing somewhat the frequency with which the shelves are read. Books taken without proper record are rarely real thefts, but nearly always borrowings to escape the limitation of rules or the inconvenience of filling out forms. Most of them come back in time, though other readers of course are handicapped in the meanwhile. The frequency of their occurrence is related to such factors as the number of day students, unobserved exits from reading rooms, the general attitude toward the library, and a number of special factors known to all librarians, such as the value of the material for professional practice. That college libraries can be operated openly without serious losses—due regard being given for these factors—has been amply demonstrated by many libraries of different sorts. Quite possibly on the admission of students to stacks losses will show some increase; but so long as these are nominal, administrators should support librarians in not taking them too seriously. A remark by the librarian of one of the most beautiful and best administered college libraries in the country is worth quoting. When the writer asked him how many books his library lost per year from its open stack system the reply was, "We don't know and do not really care. We think it's worth it in any case."[13]

[13]In L. M. Janzow, *The Library Without the Walls*, (New York: H. W. Wilson Co., 1927), there is an interesting series of reprinted articles which deal with the open shelf problem. One of these (p.191ff.) is on the loss of books resulting from this method of administering the library. I have been unable to find anything on the subject written since which examines the facts quite as thoroughly. The article's conclusions are in line with the above remarks, that in most libraries such losses viewed in terms of circulation are not serious.

CHAPTER SEVEN

Centralization versus Departmentalization

IN THE PRECEDING DISCUSSION IT HAS BEEN URGED THAT the primary effort of librarians should be directed toward making books accessible and easily used. The discussion dealt only with arrangements in the central library building. If ease of access and use, however, are to be the primary consideration, the question immediately arises whether a great many books will not be located outside the central library in places more accessible to the groups using them.

This is one of those issues which repeatedly threaten the peace and harmony of the college campus, and which the administrator is often called upon to settle. Librarians are usually to be found on the side of central housing and administration, and requests for departmental libraries are likely to be viewed as efforts to secede from the union. For the past decade or so the drift of opinion has been decidedly in this direction, as the great central library buildings so impressively witness. But there are many faculty members who still resist the march of progress and hold out for some sort of departmental collection. As Randall and Goodrich put it, "Each professor wants the books which he uses to be immediately at his hands."

The fact that the desire for some sort of library service in addition to the central library has never died down suggests that there are certain values on each side of the argument. Fortunately, there is little uncertainty concerning the factual aspects of the problem.

The case for centralization of the library resources of the institution rests on three major points:

1. First and foremost, there is the powerful argument of administrative efficiency and economy. Direct economy is achieved by (a) the avoidance of the salary costs of supervision of the additional units, (b) the avoidance of the costs of a certain amount of duplication of books involved in decentralization, and (c) the avoidance of the costs of keeping up departmental catalogs which are duplicates of portions of the union catalog. Administrative efficiency is seen in the greater expedition with which questions can be answered when all books and library staff are together under the same roof. The library is under such conditions a closer knit, more easily managed unit. This fact must be generally admitted.

2. The second point in favor of centralization is the difficulty placed by the departmental library in the way of work across departmental lines. The boundaries of a number of the departmental fields are highly artificial, and a partition of the book collection along these lines obstructs and impedes a great deal of the most fruitful sort of study and investigation. The accessibility of the books in a small collection to the department immediately concerned is achieved at the expense of its greater inaccessibility to other readers. As such collections are multiplied, the difficulties increase proportionately.

A special aspect of this difficulty is that of the undergraduate whose reading falls regularly in four or five departments. It is no doubt a convenience to such readers to be able to find what they need in one building.

3. A third point which cannot be denied is that centralization makes it possible to provide to all library users a type of library service which cannot usually be repeated in a number of locations. Reference services, general periodicals, displays of general

interest, arrangements for interlibrary borrowing, along with other facilities and services, are available in the central library. Librarians who are justifiably proud of these developments feel keenly the superiority of the service which they as librarians can render in the central building over what can be supplied in the departmental libraries.

These several considerations make up a strong case. Over against them is virtually a single argument, the desirability of getting directly at the books needed in one's work. It can be stated in strong terms. Efficiency has no meaning except with reference to the accomplishment of some particular end. In the case of the library this is the furthering of the teaching and research work of the several departments. No amount of professional skill or special library services can be as effective toward this end as the books themselves within arm's reach on the shelves. Aside from the elimination of the walk to the central building, there is brought together in the departmental library and made immediately available, material which would be scattered throughout the various rooms and floors of the central library—books, bound journals, current periodicals, pamphlets and other printed records. In such a special library the student works with all the available knowledge of his subject at his finger tips. Not only is all obstruction and delay in using the material eliminated, but there are great suggestive values in such a collection. Classics which should have been read, authorities which should be consulted, references to journals which a really thorough investigation would follow up—the volumes themselves supply daily their invitation or accusation. Nor should one overlook the ease with which the instructor can accompany the student into a departmental library located near the class room for counsel or advice. Such libraries, it is thus maintained, are educational instruments of the highest order, the loss of whose simple and direct values can be compensated for by no amount of library techniques. The argument is sometimes supplemented by pointing out that the regulations covering such collections can be adjusted more easily to fit the actual needs of readers than when they must apply to all the books and to various readers making use of the central building.

The essential truth of this general point of view, so far as it goes, can no more be denied than the difficulties first enumerated. It is clear that in the conflict of principles and interests which this problem involves there are a number of factors which vary in their relative importance from one case to another. The wise course would seem to be to appraise in each particular instance the relative importance or strength of certain of these variables. Among these the following are probably the most important:

1. How definitely circumscribed or limited are the book needs of the department requesting the separate library, that is, can it do its own work effectively in a departmental collection, or does it need constant access to a much wider collection?

2. How much is its collection needed by other groups on the campus?

3. Will the number of students, research workers, etc., to be served justify the employment of attendants for the collection, and if not, are the services of other individuals available to care for it?

4. How accessible can this material be made beneath the roof of the General Library?

Number four in this list, to work backward, embraces a great many local factors. How far from the central library is the department located? How crowded is the central library? Can satisfactory access to the material be provided there? These and other factors are often determinative. Engineering would not, for example, often be separated from mathematics and physics, but this department at Duke University is located a mile and a half from the main library and a departmental collection is indispensable. In the very large university centers where from five to ten thousand students must be served, and where congestion is very obvious, the case for breaking up the central collection to some degree seems very strong. In many other situations a re-study of the central library will reveal the possibility of freer arrangements which will meet part at least of the demand.

Variables number 1 and 2 in the preceding list will never be reduced to zero, the matter being a relative one. The connections with other departments, however, are not all of equal importance. This suggests the advisability of reading rooms to serve groups of departments rather than a single one. Departmentalization is giving way to divisional organization in many respects and in no case does this seem more likely to be advantageous than in library service. Physics, mathematics and astronomy, for example, can in most places be grouped together with great profit to the staffs of the several departments, as well as to the library administration. Certainly the biological sciences belong together. Except where a scattered physical set-up makes it difficult, a science library will ofttimes be the best answer to the pressure from science groups for departmental collections. Such a library would avoid many of the administrative difficulties of departmental collections and when coupled with a liberal policy as regards laboratory manuals and similar working tools, be more satisfactory to many readers.

The present drift of library opinion is so strongly in favor of centralization of book resources, except in the most crowded conditions, that one or two illustrations of the increase in effectiveness which can be secured in some situations by separation of subject collections from the main library, will not be out of order. One of the clearest is that afforded by the facts in connection with the establishment of the science library at Beloit College. In 1931 a room on the main floor of the science building directly opposite to the entrance was fitted up as a library. This was partly a relief measure for an overcrowded main library, partly in response to repeated faculty requests. This library included all books in the natural sciences. The librarian has supplied me with the following figures, which speak for themselves:

TABLE 28

CIRCULATION SCIENCE LIBRARY, BELOIT COLLEGE

Year	Total No. of Book With- drawals	No. of Students	Year	Total No. of Book With- drawals	No. of Students
1924-25	1,179	532	1931-32	2,090	560
1925-26	999	575	1932-33	2,098	529
1926-27	968	502	1933-34	1,914	592
1927-28	1,089	559	1934-35	1,896	525
1928-29	930	490	1935-36	2,296	560
1929-30	1,146	460	1936-37	1,896	582
1930-31	721	514	1937-38	3,092	598
7 Yr. Av.	1,004	519	7 Yr. Av.	2,183	564

The use of the science material nearly trebled the first year of the science library, with only a slightly larger student body, an increase of use due simply to the collection being made more accessible. Over a seven year period the circulation has been doubled from what it was formerly, this in spite of the fact that the science library closes at 5 P.M. while the central library had been open in the evenings also.

Further illustrations could be cited in numbers, though exact figures are often lacking. The recent experience of the School of Music of Rochester University in connection with their new library will serve as well as any other. In a year in which the arts college showed a slight decline in circulation, "the Music School," to quote the librarian, "with its new building and all its books available has shown a respectable increase, amounting to as high as 25 per cent in some of the months since the first of January."[1] Such experiences indicate the danger in a blind devotion to the policy of centralization of all resources which one sometimes meets.

It is clear from this discussion that the departmental library problem can never be settled in general terms, since one must balance general interests against special interests, consider local factors and give attention to questions of costs. There are some fields, however, in which such separate libraries will rarely be practical or desirable.[2] It is also apparent that such libraries will be less frequent in colleges of ordinary size than in larger and more complex institutions. There are two reasons for this. The first involves the factors touched upon above—the more dispersed physical plant, the larger enrolment, and the more developed graduate and research programs. The second is inherent in the character and purpose of the departmental collection. For there are two unexpressed assumptions in the departmental library idea: (a) that one wants constantly at one's fingertips all the material on a subject, and (b) that one works almost solely in one subject field. Both of these are true of graduate students and of faculty members; neither applies to undergraduates. In actual practice undergraduate use of departmental libraries is also impeded by their usual lack of facilities for handling multiple copies of

[1] The University of Rochester, *Annual Report of the Librarian, 1937-38*, p.3.
[2] Cf. G. A. Works, *College and University Library Problems* (Chicago: American Library Association, 1927), p.66ff.: "The views of faculty members were obtained in a number of institutions. . . . It was found that the great majority of those working in the humanities were opposed to this arrangement. On the humanistic side all knowledge is a unit."

reserved books, and the more limited hours during which they are open. A number of libraries can be cited in which departments with special libraries nevertheless locate their freshman-sophomore reading materials in the main library.

Thus, though departmental, divisional or special libraries will often be practical and desirable, each such proposal calls for special study of the particular facts involved. Consistent departmentalization of library resources has been tried and found wanting.[3] Departmental libraries, furthermore, will be more numerous in complex university situations than in colleges. The latter will in most cases be wiser in directing their efforts toward making the books accessible and attractive in a central building than in creating a great many departmental libraries.

But does this mean that the buildings of the college in which instruction takes place and in which the faculty members work should be bare of all books? Such a separation of instruction and study on the one hand and the literature of a subject is obviously undesirable, and it is the librarian's task and duty to bridge this gap in all practical ways. In those cases in which departmental libraries are denied, there are certain types of library service which can be supplied and which would greatly increase the vividness of instruction and the efficiency of the faculty's work. The necessity ofttimes of combatting a policy of over-departmentalization has tended to make librarians un-

[3]For the repudiation of a general policy of independent departmental libraries within a university, see the report of the faculty committee on the library problems of the University of Chicago in 1914. It is quoted in part in G. A. Works, *op. cit.*, p.73ff. For a similar repudiation of 42 departmental libraries by the faculty of Michigan State College, see the report by J. E. Towne in "Separately Shelved College-Library Collections," *Library Quarterly*, V (July, 1935), 323-40. A careful balancing of the pros and cons of the problem of centralization which appeared after the above was written is to be found in a paper by Mr. R. A. Miller, "Centralization versus Decentralization," *A.L.A. Bulletin*, XXXIII (February, 1939), 75-79. His conclusions are in virtual agreement with those above.

duly negative in their attitude toward special situations in which they could render invaluable service.

One of these situations is that in which students and instructors need to examine a certain number of books together. Unless the instructor's office is in the library building, the program is usually defeated by the physical separation of the books and the individuals most concerned with them. In such cases the obvious solution is to locate the particular books in question adjacent to the offices of the instructors. The difference between this service and a departmental library is that the latter contains all the material in the field, the former certain specified books necessary for teaching purposes. The best known development of this sort is the college Modern Language Library of the University of Chicago. This library grew out of a clearly defined objective on the part of the faculty for the elementary language courses, namely, to enable the students to read the languages studied. To this end a considerable amount of reading in the foreign language was required of each student, but the books read could be chosen in accordance with the student's own interests and tastes. For this plan to be carried out effectively, the instructor needed to advise the student at the time of his selection as to the character, content and degree of difficulty of titles considered. This could be done from a list, but was far more helpful and stimulating when done in the presence of the books themselves. The result was a consultation room and library of approximately three thousand volumes located next to the offices of the department. The collection is administered by the department members. The plan has, to quote Mr. Raney, the librarian,

resulted in highly individualized programs. A typical French class reported reading in 19 fields. Another showed 135 different works read, of which only 15 per cent were read by as many as five students while 83 books were read by a single student each. These quarters hold something besides books. There are displays, sales talks, bulletin board clipping service maintained in part by students, reading lists, newspapers and periodicals, post cards, maps, photographs, pictures, posters and other *realia*. . . . It's like getting Europe on the wire, with television.[4]

The usefulness of this library was so pronounced the University college library was modeled upon it in part. It has also suggested similar libraries elsewhere.

A development similar to the above is to be noted in the field of political science. In certain institutions courses of government have been developed which call for their students to work with the concrete forms and manuals of instruction by which governmental processes are carried on. Special rooms in which this material is located along with other documentary material, most of which is ephemeral, have proven most useful. In some locations these "laboratories in government" have contained also research materials, but not always. The Bureau of Government Research in the University of West Virginia and the Public Administration Collection at Princeton illustrate this type of arrangement. The Duke University Library is developing such a "laboratory of government."

It is also possible that a special service can be rendered to certain classes by small groups of books temporarily located in the classroom and managed entirely by the instructor. Stephens College has developed this idea rather extensively. Book cases containing from fifty to two hundred volumes stand in a number of classrooms, the books being needed during class sessions or selected by the student under the instructor's advice, or recommended for supplementary reading. They may be borrowed at the end of the

[4]M. L. Raney, "The New College Plan at the University of Chicago and Its Library," *Library Journal,* LIX (1934), 195.

class session by signing a withdrawal slip which the instructor keeps. There are all together 1,956 volumes in these several class libraries, and during 1936-37 their circulation totaled 3,690 loans, this being 12.5 per cent of the total library circulation, books in dormitory libraries excluded. The Stephens College program, which has deservedly received much attention, is not however one to be blindly imitated. It represents an aggressive acceptance of the idea that books are educational and cultural influences and an application of this philosophy to the local situation, one of the elements in which has been the lack of an adequate library building. Whether all of these class libraries justify their existence in Stephens, or would under other circumstances, might be questioned, but there is no doubt that in some instances they enable the instructor to do a better job than otherwise would be possible. The librarian's task is to determine on the one hand when this would seem to be the case, and on the other hand whether the proposal is practical from the standpoint of general library service. The points involved are fundamentally the same as in the departmental library problem already discussed, only in an easier form. Books wanted by the entire community cannot without loss be placed in a classroom and made virtually inaccessible to other users. Nor can books under heavy pressure of use even by the class be best handled in this way. But a small group of books on a very specialized subject could be charged out through the circulation desk in this manner. Where the need justifies it, duplication of a certain number of volumes is possible, particularly if reprint editions of classics can be used.

This demand for some closer contact between the instructor, the student and the literature in courses of study receives an excellent illustration in a special class library at Iowa State University. Professor Shambaugh, when asked to give a survey course on the development of modern culture, insisted on a special library for the course, located in the classroom. The collection contains approximately two thousand books, many of which are reprint editions. The room has been made comfortable and attractive by special equipment. The course is conducted by lectures, supplemented by individual reading programs made up in consultation with the instructor or his assistant. A student attendant is in charge of the room at all times. The arrangements for this course, which can scarcely be duplicated on any wholesale scale, illustrate clearly the existence of a problem with which policies of centralization, directed against the growth of departmental libraries, have failed to deal.

Before leaving the topic of special library service for particular courses of study there is one warning and one alternative solution to the problem which need to be mentioned. It is plain that the librarian who ventures into such unorthodox and unstandardized forms of library service must know what he is about. He must understand clearly the specific instructional objective he is trying to serve, as well as be aware of the purely departmental objectives which for reasons already mentioned he cannot undertake to support. He must also have a sufficiently strong position on the campus to resist demands which should not be granted. A better way of putting this perhaps is to say simply that he must have the confidence of the faculty, who are convinced that he is genuinely interested in and understands the teaching program and will do all that is consonant with general objectives to aid in carrying it out. No topic could better illustrate the need of college librarians of a different caliber than have been accepted too frequently, and of relating them to the educational, rather than the purely service aspects of the college organization.

The alternative solution to this problem proposes that classes needing special access to a group of books be transferred to the library building. In some quarters this has been expanded to the proposition that all classes in the humanities and the social sciences should meet in this building. By this means, it is urged, there will be achieved that close contact with the book collection which these courses need. The library, it is pointed out, is for these divisions what the laboratory is for the departments of natural science. At least two institutions are discussing plans for new library buildings which will have provisions of this sort. Such plans cannot be fairly discussed until they have reached a final form, and they will be awaited with much interest. Whether anyone can devise a plan, however, which will place in the library any large proportion of the class instruction without turning it into something resembling a hotel lobby or a railway waiting room remains to be proven. Foreign observers are much astonished, as it is, with the noise and confusion of American college and university libraries.[5] So far as is possible they should be kept as places of study. Offices for faculty advisors and rooms for quite small classes needing to have books accessible are certainly not impractical, but group instruction would seem to be forced into other buildings. Before bringing this herd of camels entirely into the one library tent, it is suggested that analysis of individual class book needs and experimentation in efforts to meet the actual ones in buildings other than the library, may be more desirable. The latter program has the advantage of greater flexibility at any rate, and at a time when the form of instruction is changing, this is an advantage.

There is a quite different line of attack on this problem of the separation of faculty offices and classrooms from the books which would seem to have definite possibilities, though few illustrations of its employment can be cited. There are certain books

[5]See, for example, the description of the college library "on the inside" by Wilhelm Munthe, *American Librarianship from a European Angle* (Chicago: American Library Association, 1939), p.103.

which are needed constantly in the work of a department, and there seems no real reason why a number of these should not be placed in the departmental offices. For years we have been providing those scientific departments which were without departmental libraries with several shelves of this sort of books with no deleterious effects. This has often meant some duplication, but no one can object to the duplication of material which is in constant use. A department of English literature, for example, should not have to go to the central library to verify a citation from Shakespeare or look up a reference to the King James Bible. When the new library at Columbia was built, the department of English found itself at some distance from the library, a fact which proved particularly inconvenient in answering the many inquiries which came in by mail and otherwise from the metropolitan area. The library administration accordingly placed in the offices an encyclopedia, a set of the Dictionary of National Biography and a few other works in order to enable the learned faculty to keep their dates in order and to get initials correct when they rose to instruct their classes or endeavored to enlighten the public. Such material would have to duplicate holdings in the central library, but expensive works can be avoided and older editions often used with equal satisfaction. The avoidance of duplication is often overdone. Would it not be wiser to secure additional copies of reference books and other titles used several hundred times per year than to use the same funds for new titles used perhaps once or twice? The chief difficulty seems to be the absence in most instructional buildings of any place to put such small collections. Instructional buildings seem to consist usually of classroom and individual offices. A departmental consultation room or office, where such can be arranged, could house a collection of from twenty to two hundred books which would undoubtedly serve social science and humanistic departments in the same way that laboratory handbooks have always served the science departments. Such bibliographic tools should be encumbered by virtually no rules, the departments assuming the full management of them. In the illustration above the volumes were not even listed in the union catalog. The suggestion has been made that the college librarian should have nothing to do with such collections, leaving these entirely to departmental initiative and control, or to personal acquisition. No librarian of course would want to rush into precincts where even students fear to tread, but there are several reasons why he should assume some responsibility for such collections, if desired. In the first place, such books are needed for purposes of instruction and are a proper institutional rather than personal responsibility. Nearly every professor has a study at home and should not be expected to provide a double set even of the books constantly used in his field. In the second place, the librarian can have all these books marked as property of the college, which will be a protection for them. He secures, furthermore, from time to time duplicates, which at no expense can be put to good use in such collections. Such a responsibility is also to his interest as librarian, for lacking such oversight, the collections are always liable to sudden attacks of gigantism, turning overnight into conventional departmental libraries requiring enlarged housing, supervision, and other expenditures.

Why little has been done along these lines is a natural unwillingness to trust the handling of books to the hands of anyone except the library staff. The most successful librarian, however, will be one who is able to add members of the faculty to the library staff, not in a literal way but in a program of cooperation based on mutual understanding and identity of aim. Along such a line the distinctive form of college, as distinct from public, librarianship is to be sought.

CHAPTER EIGHT

Books in Halls of Residence

IT CANNOT BE TOO OFTEN REPEATED THAT BOOKS ARE teachers, ready at a moment's notice to proclaim the truth as they possess it. They are often dull and dry, and inevitably they grow old and sometimes out of date. There are, however, certain advantages in connection with this body of teachers. They never speak except when asked to, they can be returned to silence the moment they become uninteresting, and once acquired they draw no annual stipends except the cost of the roof over their heads and a small increment of increasing cost in making room for all new comers. To these assets we who teach orally must perforce admit another advantage. This written faculty can be expanded until one can consult authorities on every subject, and, since for its faculty there is no retiring age, it can include the great scholars of the past, of whom today's leaders are proud to call themselves disciples.

The university of a century ago could be described as Mark Hopkins at one end of a log and a student at the other. Times have changed, and in the process not only the log has been replaced by elaborate structures, but informal and vital contacts between teachers and students have become more and more difficult to maintain. Efforts to recover these contacts are not unavailing, but there is one substitute for or rather supplement to the usual system which lies at hand. That is to provide students with free and informal contact with those books which experience has shown to be the best teachers. On a college campus, which exists for teaching purposes, books should be in the atmosphere.

This means not merely, as suggested above, that books should be related to classrooms, and departmental offices when specific services can be rendered without a sacrifice of other interests, but also that all practical means should be employed to bring this influence of books into the residential and more informal aspects of student life.

It is an odd fact that college and university librarians quite in contrast to their attitude toward books in buildings of instruction, have been much interested in this aspect of the library problem. Witness the great number of dormitory libraries to be found over the country and the interest of the library profession in them. The reasons for this anomaly are probably several. Librarians, always fearful of the growth of departmental libraries, have been reluctant to initiate small collections in faculty hands. Dormitory libraries, on the other hand, being for general or recreational reading, fall entirely within the librarian's own province. Not only was the librarian free from interference in working out a program along this line, but this general reading, in contrast with course reading, was his job. In this area he felt at home. Without distorting the truth, but only exaggerating it somewhat, one might say that the natural enemy of the librarian has always been the professor, not the student. Librarians are very fond of students, and will go to any lengths to interest them in books, particularly in those books of whose value they are themselves fully assured.[1] They will even locate such books outside the central library, which is the test of the big heartedness of any librarian.

[1] The writer has the following remark from the lips of the librarian of one of the important university libraries of the country: "It is not the books which the students have to read which really count; it's the books they read voluntarily."

Dormitory libraries exist in a variety of forms. They range from a dozen books on a shelf in the dormitory lobby to libraries of several thousand volumes. Some of them are beautifully housed, supervised at all times, and endowed with funds for their upkeep. A number of college presidents, baffled perhaps by the central library problem, have taken special interest in the dormitory collections and have interested others in them. Most dormitory libraries contain books chiefly of general interest and appeal, the purely recreational element being subject to considerable variation.

The theory back of these collections is, to quote the words of one library report, "that a student will pick up a book in the lounge and browse for fifteen minutes or half an hour, when she would not bother to go to the library for a book." Once interested, the book will be taken to one's room and completed. That the theory works is indicated by the reports from many such libraries.

In Pioneer Hall, a men's residence hall in the University of Minnesota, is a collection of 732 titles. About 75 volumes are in circulation on an average at all times. "The collection has entirely justified the interest shown in it by the President." Periodicals are now being added to it. In the Sanford Hall Residence Library in the same University 144 students and three faculty members were responsible for an annual circulation of 1,368, or practically 10 books to the person, this in addition to reading done from the shelves. In the Stephens College dormitory libraries are 1,993 volumes, an average of about 125 volumes to the building. An analysis of the circulation for the year 1934-35 showed that 82.95 per cent of these books circulated. The total circulation for that year was 5,311 or an average for the entire student enrolment of 7.19 per student. Since then there has been a slight decline in the circulation, the figure for 1937-38 being 4,228, which coupled with a considerable increase in the enrolment has reduced the per student average of loans considerably.[2] Just how circulation figures are to be appraised is always a question, but these figures of loans from relatively small collections would seem to justify these dormitory libraries.

Not all dormitory libraries, however, have been successful, and inquiry concerning a number of such undertakings indicates that certain generalizations can be made concerning the effective operation of them.

In the first place, the collection must either be sufficiently large to reward repeated browsing by the student or there must be the addition of new material from time to time. The one point on which all supervisors of such libraries agree is that new books must be added each year or oftener. The statement of a very competent librarian is typical of a number: "Due to the fact that we could not buy new books for the collection and the nearness of the library to the dormitories, we felt that the use of the books did not pay having the collection. However, I feel that if we could buy fifty dollars worth of new books on all subjects, we would get the books used." A worn and dog-eared collection of titles seen many times ceases to have any attraction. Where the collections are small, a system of interchange between different dormitories has been found to be useful. This is practiced at Michigan State College and elsewhere.

Experience generally seems to suggest the desirability of enlisting the aid of the students living in the several residence halls in the management of these collections. In several institutions the students have a voice in the selection of books to be added. Since distant control is largely ineffective anyhow, it is better that the enforcement of whatever rules are adopted be done by the resident group. Some sort of daily

[2]This average, however, was affected by the fact that the housing arrangements for some of the students did not provide dormitory book collections.

supervision, putting books back into place, checking up on books which the self-charging system records as having been out for an undue period, and issuing calls for books not recorded is essential. This is usually done by a student employee, and requires very little time. Book losses for these unguarded dormitory libraries seem nowhere to have been a problem. One further point must be mentioned. A number of libraries speak of the difficulty occasioned by trying to locate and call back from dormitory collections books needed for reserved use. The difficulty seems sufficiently serious to warrant the statement that all of the more serious material located in dormitories should be duplicated in the central library. On theoretic grounds this would also seem to be essential. Dormitory libraries are collections of books of general interest. Books on specialized topics might be charged out to classrooms without the risk of many calls being unsatisfied. But material of interest to the entire community should scarcely be withdrawn to be made available to only a few score possible readers.

There is one criticism to be leveled at most of these dormitory collections, and it is strange that it should be so. The great number of them make no effort at providing even simple reference tools. This is true even of certain schools which have stressed this form of library service. The cause may be that reference books are felt to be expensive and that the duplication of them in the several dormitories of the campus would be a strain on the book budget. Yet an unabridged dictionary, a one volume encyclopedia, a *World Almanac* for current figures, an *Oxford Companion to English Literature,* and one or two more books of the sort would cost less than $50, the price of 20 works of fiction. One cannot but feel that the reason for the absence of these reference tools is to be found in the point of view of the librarians responsible for them, namely, a positive appreciation of general reading coupled with a lack of a sense of responsibility for the more serious aspects of college study. The theory back of these dormitory libraries, however, would seem to indicate the special value in them of such reference books. If a boy or girl with 15 minutes to spend may not be expected to go to the library for a book, it is certainly unlikely to expect them to make the trip merely because they are uncertain over the meaning of the phrase *noblesse oblige,* or whether the American Revolution preceded or followed the French one. To build up the habit of clarifying such uncertainties is an educational contribution of the first rank. If the dormitory collections are worth doing at all—and the indications of use along with the absence of serious losses suggest that while not a substitute for the regular library program, they contribute a useful supplement—the first object of attention should be a carefully selected set of reference tools. These might vary from one residential hall to another, if students are housed according to homogeneous academic interests.

This brings one to the burning question, should such dormitory collections contain materials for assigned reading? Nothing could be more admirable, since such an arrangement places the books thought most important by the faculty right at one's bedroom or study door. Such books, furthermore, must be purchased in duplicate in any case and theoretically it would seem that some of these copies might be placed outside the main buildings. The exciting possibility suggests itself that perhaps this may be the answer to the great problem of the noise, confusion, and congestion of the average college library.

One objection on principle to the addition of such course or required readings to the residential hall library must be dealt with first. The objection was stated twice, in both cases in New England institutions of considerable reputation. In one case the statement was made by the president, in the other by the librarian. In answer to the question why such materials had not been added, the reply was, quoting one of these officials verbatim, "We feel that the reading in this library should be for pleasure." This seems to be a somewhat invidious distinction. While there are many students who are merely bored with their courses of study, if this is the view of the curriculum accepted by the institution and made the basis of its policies, the college would appear to be in a very bad way. Courses of reading are organized in the belief that they are vitally related to the development of young people. To exclude the literature of such courses from a collection on the grounds of its lack of interest would seem to be a self contradiction of the baldest sort and, if true, proof that the American college is sicker than one thought. The fact that books of travel, fiction, and detective stories may be more exciting need not be denied, but this does not mean that the systematic study of special fields of knowledge may not also be of absorbing interest. The truth of the matter is, of course, that there are some students who are eagerly interested in their work, some who are completely bored and a middle group which is moderately interested, but tends to be diverted by many other activities. It is this middle group which calls for the most careful planning, since the eager students can be depended upon to take care of themselves and the completely bored ones will probably be taken care of by the final examinations. It seems difficult to justify a college aiding in the distraction of this middle group by excluding the books involved in course reading from this most favored location, namely, at the door to one's room, in favor of the more exciting books of current interest.

But while this exclusion on principle of the more important books of the curriculum may not be justified, there are certain real difficulties of a practical character. These are chiefly two: books used in connection with courses of study are likely to be under pressure. Most dormitory libraries do not have full time supervision, and cannot therefore limit the use of particular titles so as to make them serve a number of readers at the same time. The second difficulty arises from the fact that the students registered in any particular course will be found scattered in a number of different residential halls. To provide an adequate number of copies of books required in any number of courses would require either an elaborate study of the location of students in each course or a wholesale and possibly extravagant multiplication of copies. Books for required reading will, therefore, usually have to be held in the central library building where they can be handled in such a way as to make them serve the largest number of readers. This, however, does not apply to books related to courses of study but not under the pressure of required use.

These two practical difficulties do not, however, exist in all cases, and where they are avoided a quite different policy is possible. A number of institutions provide student attendants for the residential libraries for the entire period during which they are open. In such cases and where the residential hall is large or is devoted to a particular academic group, the difficulties mentioned above are obviated. In such instances it is possible to locate in these libraries books used in courses to the great convenience of the reader and the relief of the library at its congestion point. An excellent illustration of this is the library in Burton Hall, a residential hall for men at the University of Chicago. In this large, well lighted, comfortably furnished library were placed all titles needed in connection with the four general survey courses of the college. In addition are many books of a general or recreational character. Approximately half of the titles were of this latter character. The library has been very effective. Professor Carnovsky, who made a special study of it, felt justified in making the generalization, "It is clear that from the standpoint of encouraging wide and substantial reading the dormitory library has been eminently successful."[3] The Burton Hall Library serves 390 students in a group of residence halls, and hence the University is able to provide a library service here which it does not attempt to duplicate elsewhere on the campus. Amherst College has four dormitory libraries, beautifully housed and comfortably furnished, which have complete supervision. Each such library serves a smaller number of students than does Burton Hall. One aspect of their experience in these libraries is very instructive. In a large freshman history course it was found that 75 copies of a title which all the class had to read would be sufficient when all copies were concentrated in the freshman library. If they were scattered throughout the dormitory libraries as well, 90 copies were needed. The residential situation in this case is more typical than is Burton Hall, that is, the existence of a number of dormitories, each housing a smaller group of students and requiring considerable duplication for whatever service is rendered. What the numerical "pay point" is, so to speak, which justifies providing supervision and duplication of materials needed in such locations, will depend on the state of the college finances, the number of such dormitories to be served, and what provision the institution may have made in other forms for undergraduate access to books. The average college with a scattered residential arrangement and with limited financial resources may be compelled to be content with unsupervised, small collections in dormitories, if it goes in for them at all.

This feature of American college life, which con-

[3]Leon Carnovsky, "The Dormitory Library: an Experiment in Stimulating Reading," *Library Quarterly*, III (1933), 37-65.

trasts with that of the English colleges, namely, that students are not organized in permanent residential groups, but live in buildings scattered over a large campus, changing frequently from one to the other, many of them also living in the nearby community, has impeded the development of the rather numerous dormitory libraries into a more serious form of college library service. This makes all the more interesting the recent developments at Harvard and Yale where just this subdivision of the undergraduate students into residential Houses or Colleges has been made, the groups being large enough to justify special library service for each group. These developments call for special description.

In the Harvard organization there are seven Houses. The largest of these has 299 students, the smallest 231. Each has within its own quarters its House library containing from eight to eleven thousand volumes. There are comfortable chairs and reading lamps, and smoking is permitted. The libraries are supervised at all times by student help and are open from 9 in the morning until 10 or 11 at night. The books placed there are, according to the college catalog, "practically all the books ordinarily used in tutorial work and in the large courses . . . and in addition standard reference works and well rounded collections of general literature." Reserved books for class assignments are not however placed in these libraries, but are held in the Widener Library or in one of several special reading rooms for undergraduate use which have been maintained for a number of years. The nine College libraries at Yale, ranging in size from 2,699 to 10,500 volumes, are similar in character. Required reading material is not placed in them, the pattern of the College libraries being the Linonia and Brothers open shelf reading room. Books on reserve are kept in the reserved book room of the Sterling Memorial Library.

Since all of these House or College libraries are on a completely open shelf basis, no figures can be obtained as to the circulation of books from them. However, there are certain approaches to the question so far as the Harvard libraries are concerned. A record of attendance, that is, of students using the library daily, which has, to quote the Librarian of Harvard College, "a reasonable degree of accuracy," shows a variation from an annual total of 19,000 in one House to 30,000 in another. The total for all House libraries for the year 1937-38 comes to almost exactly 175,000, or an average of 25,000 each. This figures out at a little less than an average of half of the students in each House using the library daily. This calculation must be taken in connection with another one. The official in charge of the reading room in the Widener Library reports that he cannot see that the opening of the House libraries has had any effect on the undergraduate use of the volumes placed on reserve in this room. Mr. Metcalf, the University Librarian, has also informed me that an examination of the statistics of the books borrowed from the Widener Library for home use shows a steady increase throughout the past decade, and particularly just at the time when the House libraries were opened. This can mean only one thing: this use of the House library by undergraduates represents a net gain in reading. So striking has this been that in an address before the Associated Harvard Clubs in Chicago, May 20, 1938, President Baxter of Williams College stated that "nothing in the Harvard House Plan has proved more successful than the House libraries, and nothing is more worthy of imitation." He added that the Garfield Club, the Williams College organization of nonfraternity men, had made a good start toward a working library on the Harvard model.

The values of these House and College libraries are clear enough and seem to be reflected in this evidence of increased use. Two questions are raised by these developments which are more than of local interest. In the first place, there is the very practical question whether it is wise to develop undergraduate library service by means of a number of House or College libraries supplemented by the reading rooms for freshmen and other special libraries or to develop a single undergraduate or college library. The latter, it will be recalled, was suggested as one of the ways by which undergraduates in crowded universities could be given direct access to the books which they need most frequently. The system of residential hall libraries is an alternative solution to the problem. The single college library would be more economical, and would permit the collection of a larger supply of materials than is possible in each of the residential halls. One thinks of the files of the more important periodicals, for example, or of recent census reports, which one would not like to duplicate in a number of residential halls. On the other side it can be urged that the residential hall libraries, for institutions which can finance them, go a full step further in making books accessible to students and in interesting them in reading, while at the same time requiring their attendance at the central library for the use of periodical files, government documents and other materials too expensive or too seldom used to warrant duplication. Between these alternatives no universally applicable choice probably is to be made. Local factors enter in, such as the dispersion of the undergraduate living quarters, the number of day students, the extent to which the undergraduates of the institutions have the habit of buying books, and the like. For those institutions which can afford the larger cost it must be admitted that the presence of a library of nine or ten thousand volumes in the residence hall itself has a great attraction, provided routines can be established for eliminating useless volumes and keeping the collections alive. The general library would carry in such cases the serials and other materials which should not be duplicated. In the case of Harvard it is only fair to add that in certain fields both methods are used: The Boylston Hall Reading Room is really a college library for classes in history, economics, and government. Special reading rooms in literature, classics and other subjects are also to be found in the Widener Library or in other buildings in Harvard Yard.

This leads to the second question raised by these libraries. At present they do not include the books required for regular class readings, though the House libraries at Harvard include books needed for tutorial assignments and for the reading period. This may be due at Harvard, in part, to the effectiveness of the special libraries which have for some years supplied reserved books to undergraduates in their fields. At both Harvard and Yale, however, the regular class reserves are to be found in the main library or in other centrally located libraries. This would seem to indicate that the undergraduate library program in neither institution has yet been fully integrated or defined. It is of course true that reserves can be placed at any place where they can be easily handled and students can get at them, and the matter is one of practical convenience rather than of moral principle. Nevertheless, if convenience of access justifies the establishment of these fully supervised College and House libraries, there would seem to be little logical reason for leaving at the central building the books most frequently needed and in which the assignments are most specific. Duplication of these books is essential in any case, and while more copies will be required if the copies are dispersed, the additional cost will scarcely bankrupt either of the universities in question. The central library would continue to serve the student for special papers or investigations and for all the volumes needed which his own library would not provide. That the subdivision of this required reading into a number of smaller and quieter units would in itself be an unmitigated gain, can scarcely be questioned. To an outsider it would seem that the tradition of the gentleman's library has influenced the conception of those libraries to an observable degree. It would seem, however, no impairment of even a gentleman's library to have in it the books needed most. If there are inherent difficulties in placing the most essential books in residential libraries, it would seem that the plan of a single college library adequately staffed to handle undergraduate reading may appear in the long run to be the wiser solution to the problem.

The importance of this topic is not so much with reference to the two institutions which have systematically developed these libraries, for it may well be that there are local or temporary factors, either of a practical nature or of student tradition, which are responsible for the special character of the collections. The attention given to the point is warranted only by the fact that these House and College libraries loom as possible patterns for a new form of library service for undergraduate colleges existing in university centers. This possibility rests on the fact that on the one hand ten to twelve thousand volumes can provide for the constant needs of most undergraduates if these are supplemented by the great reserves of a university library, while on the other hand nothing is so destructive of the atmosphere of study or the usefulness of a library as the massing of hundreds of undergraduate readers at one spot to make brief and hurried use of a number of books. The residential form of college organization, which breaks up the student body into groups, each large enough to warrant separate library service, offers one way out. It is one which can be used, however, only by institutions able and willing to provide the somewhat larger costs involved.[4]

There is one other residential unit in American college life for which library facilities should be encouraged—the college fraternity. A good deal has been done along this line, and the lines of this service seem fairly clear.

College fraternities are continuing bodies each with a strong sense of its corporate life and service, and an ability to discipline its members. They can therefore operate their own libraries with reasonable effectiveness. Where the fraternity has its own house, this library may develop considerable proportions, especially with the aid of alumni members. Such collections obviously serve the smaller group of brothers in the same way that dormitory libraries in general are useful. The fact that the fraternity library will be purchased and maintained by the group itself, thus relieving the college library to a certain extent, is a further ground for giving it attention and support.

There are several things the library can do in aid of these collections. In the first place, guidance can be given as to the books which will prove most useful, particularly in the case of reference tools.[5] The order department can advise the fraternity library committee where and how to buy, or do the buying for them. Such aid is particularly useful if the fraternity is compelled by shortage of funds to purchase encyclopedias or other reference sets at second hand. At

[4]Cf. the remarks of Mr. Willis Kerr, librarian of Claremont College: "Ideally if we could begin again at the beginning of library provision for Pomona and Scripps, perhaps we would develop a working library in each hall of residence, each library in part at least a duplicate of others. The most expensive reference and periodical sets would be concentrated in a central library for each college or for the group of colleges. Almost this plan of library development has obtained at the eight Selly Oaks Colleges in Birmingham, England." —"Report of the Harper Hall Dedication Conference," *Claremont Library Series*, No. 1 (1932), p.14.

[5]The Pennsylvania State College Library compiled a list of seven hundred books which it called "The Fraternity Five Foot Shelf." The interfraternity council, with which the library maintained a close cooperation in this matter, published five hundred copies of this list.

Pennsylvania State College, for example, the library bought the books for fraternity libraries, thus securing for them the library discounts and savings in transportation costs.[6] This library also provided and inserted a suitable bookplate and instructed the fraternities in a simple method of cataloging. The objections usually raised to buying the books at a discount are the possibility of personal orders being run in on the general fraternity list, and the overhead cost of a great many small orders placed throughout the year. Aside from the fact that some additional book buying by undergraduates would do neither them nor the college any harm, these difficulties can be controlled by (a) eliminating textbooks and other obviously individual items from the list, and (b) accepting such lists for purchase only at stated times.

Several colleges have experimented successfully with certain special services to these fraternity house groups of students. The Olin Library at Wesleyan University operates for the fraternity houses a system of traveling libraries. Each library consists of 25 or 30 books, including both fiction and nonfiction, and these are rotated through the several fraternities every two months. The fraternities agree to give the books shelf-room and safekeeping, and to contribute 3 books annually to the common pool. The University of Oregon operates a loan system by which 10 to 15 books are charged out to the fraternity. These remain until the fraternity librarian notifies the library that the fraternity wants these changed.

It goes without saying that a similar service would be rendered to nonfraternity residential groups whenever possible. The difficulty, of course, is that without some continuing organization the arrangements made break down at the end of the year. Where some organization exists, it may be possible to give even

[6]Jackson E. Towne, "Separately Shelved College-Library Collections," *Library Quarterly*, V (1935), 338ff.

greater assistance to such a group because of its larger number. The development of a residential library patterned on the House library of Harvard by the Garfield Club, the nonfraternity group at Williams College, has already been mentioned.

These various efforts to relate books to the living quarters of students are all to the good, but when everything has been said, the fact remains that the most effective library of all is the one which the student owns himself.[7] In this respect American college students show up very badly in comparison with those of European institutions. Book buying by undergraduates is confined largely to required textbooks. This is a result in part no doubt of the class system of instruction, the student having received the impression that his chief task was to assimilate the contents of the text. It is due in part also to our democratic system of education which has brought to college campuses thousands of students who have no real literary interests. So far as the libraries are concerned we seem to be at a transition point. The textbook system of college teaching has been modified, in part, into a sort of continuous text, required of all students, printed in a number of books, with the library furnishing the texts. The shift toward greater freedom in study and more adjustment to individual needs is under way, but it is not clear how far it will go. In the meanwhile it is quite possible that students are required to buy fewer books than when all courses were of the textbook type. No one can doubt, however, the desirability of students purchasing for their own use not only their textbooks, but the more important books in their several fields of study—whatever books

[7] In "The Manual of Instructions and Exercises" for the English A course at Harvard, after an enumeration of the various libraries available to the freshmen students, appears the following pertinent word of advice: "Nevertheless it is often true that the most valuable library for any college student consists in the few dozen or few hundred books that he owns himself. Every student ambitious to distinguish himself as a reader and a writer ought to begin buying books."

in fact they need to know thoroughly. Out of such possession comes not only a great saving of time and nervous energy to the student and of actual cost to the library, but also the continuous educational effect of books on one's desk and beside one's bed.

The college bookstore, in other words, is from a broad standpoint an essential part of the library, or better still, of the college educational system. In so far as it is a purveyor of materials for learning, a college would seem justified in operating it on the same basis as it does its chemical supply store. That the control and direction of the bookstore should be in the hands of the college itself is axiomatic. A close correlation with the library is very desirable, and the librarian should be one of the members of the managing board. One practical aspect of such a correlation is the possibility of disposing of duplicates acquired by the library through the proper book selling agency of the campus. Negatively, this correlation would avoid the possibilities which may be illustrated from one campus visited during the year, where the proposal of the library to install a rental collection of textbook materials was opposed and blocked by the bookstore for commercial reasons. To permit commercial objectives to come into the college program at this point—except perhaps for current fiction, detective stories and other purely recreational materials —would seem more difficult to defend than at almost any other point.

That the bookstore and the library have a common objective and should be operated in the same spirit is not merely a beautiful theory, but has been demonstrated as quite practical by a number of institutions. The beautiful Cooperative Bookshop of Vassar College is an excellent illustration of what can be done along this line. The store is located on the first floor of the building in which the post office and other centers of student interest are to be found. It is cooperative in the full sense, being owned by its members. Membership is open to students, faculty, alumnae, and employees of the college. The board of directors consists of five students, three faculty members, and the manager of the Bookshop. The college subsidizes it by allowing free rent, light and heat. "In exchange for these privileges, the Bookshop is expected, by having books and other educational materials easily accessible to the college community, to be an integral part of the intellectual life of the college. A large inventory of books is carried and any member of the community may consult them. No attempt is made to force sales." In addition to books, a large stock of framed pictures is carried for rental purposes, the Department of Art being responsible for the choice of the pictures. It also operates a rental collection of phonograph records chosen by the Music Department. It is contrary to the policy of the Bookshop to publish figures of its sales and dividend returns except to its members, but it may be said that it does a thriving business. It is, without question, one of the most stimulating places on the campus.

In addition to the study of the general circulation which has already been referred to, Professor Eurich of the University of Minnesota also made a detailed study of the reading of 317 undergraduates.[8] One of the points discovered was that less than 25 per cent of the total time spent in reading was done in the University library building. A library program which does not recognize the fact that undergraduates spend more time in their residence halls than they do in the library building, and does not endeavor by all practical means to bring into these halls the atmosphere of reading and intellectual inquiry, will fail in part of its cultural mission. As remarked above, on a college campus books should be in the atmosphere.

[8] A. C. Eurich, "Improvement in Scholarship During the Probationary Period," *School and Society*, XXXVI (January, 1932), 92-96.

CHAPTER NINE

How Large Should the College Library Be?

THE USUAL MEASUREMENT OF A LIBRARY'S EFFECTIVE-
ness is how many books it contains. The simplicity of
this summary together with the American tendency to
form such quick quantitative judgments, has lead to
an emphasis on the mere size of the book collection
which is all out of proportion to the significance of
the fact. Libraries have been rated in various lists by
the number of their volumes. Much more influential
has been the fact that the standards of certain accrediting agencies as regards libraries have been stated
in terms of number of volumes, quite irrespective of
what the books are. The absurdity of this procedure—
for which librarians, be it noted, have not been responsible—is made fairly luminous when one receives
requests, as the writer has on two occasions, from small
college libraries for gifts of books in order to swell
the holdings to the number specified by the accrediting agency. Any books which could be counted would
serve, it was baldly stated. The struggling college
would then find it necessary, of course, to spend its
money to catalog and house the books, which in such
cases would be likely to be of such a character as to
serve no educational purposes. Happily, most accrediting agencies have recently or are in process of modi-
fying their requirements in these respects.

Apart from a tendency to rank libraries according
to the number of their volumes and the pressure of
accrediting agencies, the factor most responsible for
policies of gross accumulation has probably been the

feeling that every book contains something of value and should be preserved. This is an insidious argument because of the element of truth which it contains. Most librarians have discovered that it is really impossible to prove that any given piece of paper with writing on it will have no value for research studies of the future. The Oxyrhynchus papyri, which have been of the utmost historical importance, are, for example, personal letters, housewives' shopping lists and other ephemera recovered from the rubbish heaps of that small town west of the Nile. The dime novels of a generation ago are now being collected, and the handbills about local amusements and even patent medicine advertisements of a century ago may be material of great use for the social historian.

A case can be made out for the possible usefulness of every book and its inclusion in the library. This fact, coupled with an ignorance on the part of faculty members and even administrative officers as to the cost of cataloging, preserving and servicing an enlarging collection, has led too often to a policy of adding to the collection any and all books on which hands could be laid, in the belief that thereby the library is being enriched. It is obvious, however, that a book which will not be used is a liability rather than an asset, increasing by its presence the cost of all routine processes and obscuring the presence of books which ought to be read. While one might admit that it is desirable to have all books preserved, certainly this service to the scholarship of the future is not one which most college libraries can afford. That is a function of the national library and, in particular fields, of special and university libraries. The function of the college library, and usually its financial exigencies as well, confine it to the preservation of books for its teaching program and for the direct use of faculty members in study and research. The exceptions to this rule are generally recognized. Every college library has an obligation to acquire simply for purposes of preservation the records of its own institutional history, and, if the material is not being collected by other agencies, the more important records of the local community and possibly of the agency or organization by which it is supported.

Two developments in recent years have made a policy of indiscriminate accumulation on the part of the small college even more unnecessary and extravagant than was the case a few decades ago. The first has been the interlibrary loan movement. Practically every large library now makes its resources available—certain classes excepted—to all serious readers in other libraries. The loan usually is completely free, only the transportation costs of the books being asked, though the actual cost to the lending library of clarifying the often incomplete or incorrect title requested and of withdrawing and mailing the book, far exceeds the item of transportation cost. The liberality and value of these now quite general arrangements cannot be overstated. They represent a major contribution by librarians to the development of scholarship and enlightenment, a contribution which is to be ranked with the services of other professions to the public good. This free access for serious readers everywhere to the book collections of the great libraries makes it unnecessary for the small college library to undertake to preserve volumes merely because of a possible but improbable need for them. Such volumes should be donated to a nearby university library. The second development supplements these general loan arrangements, namely, the development of microphotography. One of the older difficulties in supplementing a library's holdings by means of interlibrary loans was that certain classes of material were often withheld from such arrangements, for example, periodical volumes in the Library of Congress. The largest libraries now provide facilities, by which single articles in journals or excerpts from books which the library might not wish to lend may be microfilmed for a few cents and mailed to the reader in an ordinary envelope.

These developments have raised the question as to whether there is any necessity for the college library to be as large as used to be thought necessary for respectability. Strong support for this point of view has come from another quarter, the realization that undergraduate use of college libraries in general has not been very great. If only a small portion of the book collection is used, why, it is being asked, should colleges build up these large libraries?

On this last point new and impressive data have recently been secured in the study by Mr. H. L. Johnson, of student reading in five colleges. This study was referred to in Chapter II above, and the data dealing with the number of volumes used per student reviewed. Mr. Johnson also examined the reading records from the standpoint of the number of volumes used and their frequency of use. The record is for one academic year, the enrolments in the five institutions ranging from 238 to 675. In the case of one of the colleges, figures were not available for the reserved book usage. The total number of volumes available in the five libraries was 345,000 volumes. According to Mr. Johnson's report there were used 17,012 volumes from the general collection of the five libraries and 3,774 volumes from the reserved book collection of four libraries. Thus all five colleges (reserved usage in one college excepted) used only 20,786 books. If this missing reserved use could be assumed to have been the maximum reported by the other four colleges—and the college in question was below the maximum reported in general reading—the total number of volumes used would have been 22,537. The largest number used by any one of the four colleges for which the figures are complete was 7,601 volumes.

There were a number of very striking facts turned up in this study. Perhaps most startling was the very limited number of titles which were used in every one of the colleges. From the general collections, only 30 titles were used in all 5 of the colleges, and from the reserved book collections of the four colleges supplying these data, only 7 titles. Also of interest was the fact that the median number of withdrawals of those titles placed on reserve which were used at all, was 12.4, a fact which led Mr. Johnson to the conclusion that the college libraries are supplying textbooks to students. This heavy use of volumes placed on reserve contrasts with the fact that of the loans from the general collections 11,502 titles or 67.61 per cent of the total were used only once. The point of immediate interest, however, is the primary fact that instead of 345,000 volumes, a collection of 25,000 volumes *correctly selected* would have served the undergraduate needs for the year of all five colleges, reference materials excepted, and 10,000 volumes would have taken care of any one of the colleges. Of the total number of volumes available only 6.5 per cent were used during the year.

This study is the most complete that has been done along this line, though lesser studies had already pointed to the same results. The obvious question arises: If in a single year the students in a college such as those studied uses only 7,500 volumes, why should the library house and service 75,000?

Thus a reaction against the large library has been gathering force. It is being suggested in some circles that the basic conception of the college library has been wrong, and that instead of imitating its university neighbor, it should hold its library to a working collection, eliminating books to make room for new ones whenever the collection rises above some set figure. One of the best known writers on college library problems suggested recently in an address that the college library of the future will be a continually changing collection of about 25,000 volumes.

This is a challenging and provocative proposal. As a general expression of the conviction that a small collection of books pertinent to the courses of study is more valuable than a larger haphazard collection, it is to be highly approved. Professor Ayres, for example, writing of the Reed College Library some years ago, when it was smaller than at present, had the following statement to make about it:

"The best working library for undergraduates that I have ever known was that of Reed College. The library like the College was young. Like the College it was almost completely free from the dead hand of tradition. It contained nothing but what was fresh and live and useful to the generation that was using it."[1]

This is a very effective reminder of the fact that size does not make a college library either stimulating or efficient, and that the refusal to add books unrelated to the program of work achieves not only economy, but certain positive gains. The usual problem, however, in connection with keeping libraries small arises from the fact that few of them are built up within a short period. They are rather the results of book buying over a period of years by many different individuals. They contain inevitably many volumes dealing with problems no longer of active interest, or approaches to subject fields which the present faculty members no longer pursue. The proposal that the college library should be a changing collection of 25,000 volumes aims to secure this working collection of pertinent material by withdrawing infrequently used books in sufficient numbers to keep within the limits set. As a program of specific action the proposal faces certain serious difficulties.

In the first place it is extremely difficult to determine what is "dead wood" and what is not. Certain

[1]*Reed College Bulletin,* XV, No. 4 (November, 1936).

classes of books offer no problem—out-of-date textbooks, duplicate copies no longer needed, books of
sermons and theological works donated by ministerial
friends of the institution, isolated volumes of public
document series, and earlier editions of many works.
The systematic removal of such material will be to
the general profit of the library. But beyond such
categories, determining what will not be needed is
extremely difficult. To rely upon actual use within a
period of several years would be to adopt the danger-
ous policy of reducing the library to items of immediate interest. A change of faculty members might bring
back a demand for material which has been undis-
turbed for a number of years. For one reason or another books which readers seem to have passed by
come back into circulation. Although efforts to secure
objective data on the number of books which circulate
again after several years' neglect were usually baffled,
figures were secured from one library. The Tulane
University Library changed their system of book pockets about 10 years ago, but instead of reworking the
entire book collection at once the pockets have been
inserted as these older books have been called for.
Books which had not been taken from the library for
ten years were thus apparent. The circulation department states that from 2 to 15 books of this character
have been loaned daily from the circulation desk. In
a daily circulation of from 75 to 110 volumes this
represented from 2.6 to 13.6 per cent of the general
circulation. Certainly in this institution the complete
removal of all books not used for 10 years would have
been a mistake.[2]

A second difficulty is that this proposal to limit the
college library to a small collection of current interest

[2]The possibility of securing some light on the problem by utilizing
this situation at Tulane was suggested to me by Mr. Helmer Webb,
librarian of Union College. Other libraries which can throw light on
the problem owing to some similar arrangement will render a service
by publishing the figures for their institutions.

will probably impede the sort of instruction which endeavors to stimulate individual investigation and inquiry. Where such inquiry will lead no librarian or faculty committee can say in advance. Whether a library of 25,000 volumes could support the Princeton plan of instruction, in which juniors and seniors do the equivalent of one course in special studies of their own choosing is very doubtful. At Wesleyan University seniors are required, as in a number of other schools, to write theses. In 1936-37 there were 45 of these. A count of the number of titles listed by them in their bibliographies showed an average of fifty titles. Faculty estimates of the number of titles consulted by them but not listed, placed the figure at twice the number in the lists. Since these were all highly specialized studies, there was very little duplication of titles between them. In other words, to quote Mr. Rider, the librarian, "our senior Honors students alone for their theses used this year somewhere around six thousand titles, the majority of them naturally of an extremely specialized character." In efforts to get students to verify statements of secondary authorities by consulting the original sources, the limitations of a small library will also be felt. Thus while the small collection would no doubt serve the majority of students in most institutions quite satisfactorily, it militates against the best students and what seems increasingly regarded as a necessary element in the best method of instruction. It would be a mistake to conceive of the library's task in terms of the average student rather than of the best.

A library of 25,000 volumes is no doubt easier to work in, and it may be highly desirable in the larger institutions to provide either special reading rooms or college libraries with small collections, as has been suggested. But students in such cases will always have access to the main library to supplement their more accessible collections. To confine their work for all four years to a small number of books would seem to be possible only in institutions where the students' work is very definitely specified. Nor is the argument of economy as strong as it appears at first sight. Owing to the fact that we catalog our books so elaborately, it costs practically as much money to get a book out of the library as the shelf space it occupies is worth. Estimates given by catalogers as to how rapidly this work of tracing and withdrawing all cards can be done, show that it costs somewhere between 15 and 25 cents per title to get a book out of a library. The cost of shelf space works out to be about 25 cents per volume.[3] Of course, where free time of some member of the library staff can be utilized for this work, an immediate economy can be achieved. Otherwise, under present cataloging schedules, it seems to be just about as cheap to build additional stacks as to get books out of a library, once they have become parts of it. The saving to the library in sharply reducing the book collection would be in the greater economy of all subsequent operations. This will be a real saving, but one that it is impossible to estimate.

To sum up this discussion: An arbitrary limit to a college library fixed at a point which involves eliminating all except the immediately active material seems to create more problems than it solves. Discarding should be as constant and as normal a process as additions, but it would seem wiser to let this be determined by the uselessness of the material or its availability in a nearby institution rather than by a determination to keep the library small. Whatever may be practically necessary, the ideal would seem to be to have available all books vitally related to the subjects of the curriculum that can be secured. That the volumes are not used in one, two or five years is not proof that

[3] I am indebted to Mr. Louis F. Stagg, vice-president of Snead and Company, for this figure. He emphasizes, however, that this result should be treated only as "the roughest and crudest sort" of estimate.

they are not needed, since the questions addressed to a library in one year will not be identical with those of another year. Although there may be an upper limit to the proper size for a college library, no two people will probably agree what this figure is. All sorts of local factors will affect the figure. The several points which seem undebatable are (a) the desirability of eliminating numerical goals in either direction, (b) the continual removal of books which have obviously ceased to be of value, and (c) expansion only on the basis of need and actual use.[4]

[4]It might be of interest for college administrators to check occasionally on the use of books bought in response to special requests or grants. Two institutions have reported a check made on the use of books bought with funds from Carnegie grants. In both cases about half the books bought with these funds had not been taken from the library. The names of these institutions are not even recorded in the files of this project, and its director is rapidly forgetting them.

CHAPTER TEN

What Books Should the Library Buy?

EVERYTHING WHICH HAS BEEN SAID EMPHASIZES THE importance of book selection. The fact that a small library intelligently selected is a better library than a larger one chosen without much discrimination, makes it easily possible for a college to overcome a financial handicap by careful planning. Attention to the question is even more imperative for larger institutions, since the limited book funds of the small college automatically impose a high degree of selection in the acquisition of books.

What books should be bought? It is easy to frame an answer in general terms—those books which aid the faculty in their teaching and in their studies or research undertakings. In addition, there will be some volumes of general literature and the more important reference books. Such general statements are not very helpful, however, when one comes to particulars.

Since most liberal arts colleges teach the same broad subjects, it might seem possible to prepare a list of the books which an ideal college library should contain. A number of such lists have been prepared. The best known of these, *The List of Books for College Libraries* (compiled by Charles B. Shaw) contains about 14,000 titles.[1] Others calling for special mention are: Horton, Marion, *Buying List of Books for Small Libraries* (1935), Hester, Edna A., *Books for Junior Colleges* (1931), and Mohrhardt, Charles B., *List of Books for Junior College Libraries* (1937).

[1] A seven-year supplement (1931-38) will be published by the American Library Association early in 1940.

These lists have been of very great value. They have enabled colleges to inspect their own holdings and have served as buying guides in many instances. None of these lists, however, can in any sense be regarded as definitive, for the reason that effective buying must be related to the program of work which is being undertaken in each particular institution. A proof of this fact is clearly presented in the case of the Shaw list. Before its publication it was checked against the holdings of 96 college libraries. The largest number of books in the list found in any one of these libraries was 8,251 or 58 per cent. The lower limit was 158 titles or 1.1 per cent. The average for the entire group was 18 per cent of the titles in the list.[2] The fact that very few colleges had found it necessary to have more than sixty per cent of the titles in the list must be due in the main to the extensive variations in the actual handling of the same general subjects of instruction in different colleges. One sees readily how this would be so. In the teaching of literature, for example, the importance attached by one group of instructors to historical antecedents, or to social background, would result in considerable buying, the need for which would not be felt to that degree in other institutions. Differences of method of instruction will also affect to some extent the titles to be acquired. That this is the explanation of the lack of agreement among libraries as to what books should be bought is suggested also by the experience of the compiler in preparing this list. A preliminary list of titles was made up largely on the basis of Swarthmore usage, and sent to a selected group of teachers over the country. To

[2]Charles B. Shaw, *A List of Books for College Libraries* (2d prelim. ed. Chicago: A.L.A., 1931), p.v. Subsequent checking widened the range of holdings discovered. Dr. Bishop at the dedication of the Harper Hall Library in 1932 reported that the range of holdings was from 158 to nearly 90 per cent of the titles. The average of all institutions checked, however, was only 2,700 titles or 19 per cent. See Willis Kerr, "Report of the Harper Hall Dedication Conference," *Claremont Library Series*, No. 1 (1932), p.24.

quote from the Preface of the completed volume: "Because of such disparities in the recommendations received, the list was rearranged in three sections representing different degrees of uniformity of judgment on the part of those consulted."

One of the results of the study of the reading of five colleges by Mr. H. L. Johnson which has already been cited in another connection bears on this point. Mr. Johnson checked on the number of titles which were used during the academic year of his study in all of the colleges. Had some uniformity of use been discovered, it would have suggested the possibility of a college book list made up on this practical basis of actual use. Mr. Johnson found, however, only 30 titles used in common from the general collections of the 5 colleges and only 7 from the 4 reserved book collections. The explanation of this surprising fact need not at present detain us. It suggests a considerable dependence in these institutions on textbooks and secondary sources of which there are many, one about as good as another for the purpose. Whatever the explanation may be, however, the implications of this study are decidedly negative from the standpoint of a master book list made up on the basis of actual borrowings.

These facts indicate that no list can be prepared which should be blindly followed by all institutions, though the value of those available in suggesting titles and in distracting attention from the current best sellers cannot be minimized. The fact that their proper use is suggestive, however, relieves one of the necessity of debating which is the best list to be followed. All of the more important ones should be at hand and be consulted by those responsible for the book selection.

Each college library thus is thrown back on the necessity of making its own book selection. The question immediately arises as to who should do this. A variety of schemes are to be found in the different colleges and universities. They place the responsibility variously on the three agencies: the librarian, a library committee, and the members of the faculty, the usual unit in the last case being the department.

Into such a problem as this local and personal factors enter heavily, yet certain general principles can be seen amid the diversity of methods employed.

The first and most indisputable one is that the librarian must be finally responsible for the book buying program, and in order to be held responsible must have the right to veto or hold up any purchases which he feels to be undesirable. The necessity for this is seen when one recalls how easily and frequently departments or individuals may adopt policies which are completely out of line with those of the library as a whole. An illustration which may seem extreme but which is an actual case may be cited. A department of forestry in an eastern university, whose library materials were located in a reading room with those of the other biological departments, was found to be buying duplicate copies of books already on the shelves of the reading room. On inquiry it was frankly admitted that this duplication did not rest on readers' demand but was to insure a complete set of duplicates of all books in which the department was interested, this in preparation for a future independent library for the department. No such separate library being anticipated by anybody else on the campus, at least in the near future, this admittedly needless duplication was promptly ended by the librarian. Other misuses of book funds could be cited, such as book buying for personal rather than academic purposes—one of the best collections on stock breeding in the South is to be found in the library of a normal college, whose president had a large farm near the campus—excessive duplication of copies far beyond the accepted standards, or a use of book funds for research purposes to the neglect of student needs in the field. Though these misuses of the funds are not numerous, some unifying force is a necessity if any general policies are to be established, and this is the librarian's proper responsibility. Faculty members, it must be remembered, are individualists by nature and training, and it could easily happen that in 25 or more departments the policies followed, were there no such central control, could easily conflict with one another.

It is obvious, however, that no librarian can select books in the sense of originating the orders in more than a very few fields. In a larger university where it is possible to have a number of subject specialists on the library staff it may be possible for this to be done by such a group. We shall return to this point later. In the case of the college or average university library, however, the specialized personnel is lacking. The selection would devolve upon the librarian alone, usually with the assistance of not more than one or two others. In such instances the ability or competence of the library staff to choose the books to be bought is definitely limited. Nor can a library committee suggest the titles to be purchased outside the fields of specialization of its members any more successfully. The work of originating the book orders falls necessarily upon the various subject specialists of the faculty. The real problem, therefore, so far as the bulk of the buying is concerned, is twofold: by what method and on what basis shall the book funds be apportioned to the various individuals or departmental groups, and, secondly, if the work of selection is thus to be performed by a large number of individuals, how can any standards or policies in book buying be maintained? These two questions will have to be considered separately.

There is a strong feeling on the part of many librarians that the book funds should be placed entirely in the hands of the librarian, leaving him to allocate these from year to year in accordance with his knowledge of actual needs. Certain practical considerations are cited in support of this view. The book needs of different instructional departments vary from year to year, due to changes in personnel and other factors. The librarian, it is urged, should be in a position to modify the allotments to these different groups in accordance with these fluctuating needs. The method of having more or less fixed allotments to each department is attacked on the ground that any such schedule encourages some groups to spend money merely to avoid losing it at the end of the year, while other groups are suffering from lack of funds. The extreme form of this procedure is one in which the librarian allots book funds to faculty members individually, rather than to departments. Where this procedure obtains, the librarian decides not only which departments need money but also the individuals within the departments who shall be given the right to spend it.

The best administrative procedure depends so much on local factors, and in particular on the personal qualifications and qualities of the librarian, that no one would want to insist on a uniform practice in all libraries. No doubt also a tactful and competent librarian who has won the confidence and respect of his faculty can work successfully under almost any system. It may be of use, however, to point out some of the difficulties which attend the practice of placing all funds at the personal disposal of the librarian and load it with dangers, particularly for the official himself.

In the first place, it is extremely difficult for the librarian to determine the relative book needs of a department or individual—except perhaps as regards the number of duplicate copies needed—with sufficient exactness to enable him to make with safety sharp and radical distinctions from year to year in the amounts allocated from the book funds. In actual practice needs are too likely to be determined by the persistence and vigor with which the various individuals press their claims. The meek are not likely to inherit the college book funds. An unexpressed feeling that funds for books are secured either by being the friend of the librarian or by starting a rumpus is too likely to grow up. The faculty member asking for book funds under this system is put in the position, or, rather, feels himself in the position, of one asking a favor of the librarian. After one or two refusals, even though there be good reasons for them, he is too likely to refrain from further requests. These are not imaginary dangers; actual situations where they exist can be cited. Uncertainty as to funds which will be available, furthermore, prevent planning of the growth of a departmental book collection from year to year. All of this means a loss of interest in the library and is likely to be accompanied by efforts to secure funds directly from the administration or by the levying of special class funds. A system of regular departmental allotments seems to have a good deal more in its favor, provided that the allotments are well within the limits of assured need, and that these departmental allotments never exhaust the entire book fund.[3]

In determining the percentages of the funds to be allotted annually to each department the librarian will certainly wish to act with or through the library committee. Several factors enter in, the size of the department, the amount of research work being carried on, and the character of the library materials themselves being perhaps the most important. No formula

[3]A third alternative of having the book funds expended *in toto* by a library committee probably has less to commend it than any other. Such a committee suffers from the facts that the primary attention of its members is directed toward other matters, is likely to lack continuity of action because of a changing personnel and, partly for this same reason, has something of the irresponsibility of all group action. Such bodies, however, as will be remarked, are invaluable in an advisory capacity.

has yet been evolved which makes any claim to include all of these. The one in use at Duke University
—a division of one third of the departmental funds
equally among all departments and two thirds in proportion to the student enrolment—worked very satisfactorily so long as the institution was largely an
undergraduate college. It represents a reasonable com-
promise between the claims of large and small departments, but does not take into consideration some of
the other factors involved which, consequently, have
to be cared for by means of the general or undis-
tributed funds. Mr. G. Flint Purdy, the librarian of
Wayne College, has made a detailed study of the factors affecting the book needs of the several departments of his institution, but writes that he does not
believe any single formula covering all the factors can
be evolved which would not be so complicated that
only the mathematicians would understand it. It must
be admitted, therefore, that any regular system of
allotments will be only a rough approximation of
justice, rather than a refined and absolute standard.
Nevertheless some rough principle of regular allotments is certainly less arbitrary, particularly if supplemented and corrected by additional grants from
the unallocated funds, than to leave the departments
with no assured funds and dependent on the fluctuating favor of the librarian. It has already been urged
that funds so allotted should be expended in line with
general library policies and subject to the librarian's
approval.

It has been remarked that in no case should all of
the funds available be divided among the departments. Not only must the reference collection be kept
up, other general items purchased and emergencies be
met, but there is the constant need of items which
exceed in cost the amount which it would be wise to
allocate regularly to the various departments. It is
thus highly desirable that there should be a fund for

which items of outstanding importance can be secured, items such as Migne's *Patrologiae* or a file of
the *Spectator*. In the selection of such items to be
bought by means of the general fund, the librarian
needs the advice of the faculty library committee,
both to aid him in appraising the value of titles suggested, and to share the responsibility of expending
fairly considerable sums for sets which will not be
used very frequently. The justification of the latter
is of course that such items are like high grade bonds:
though their yield may be low in a single year, they
will continue to return dividends in use year after
year without fail.

In these suggestions it may be felt that the librarian
is assigned an ignominious role. For the regular departmental allotments his favor does not need to be
solicited, and in the purchase of larger items he
should seek the library committee's advice, if not
their consent. This is quite different from the situation of which librarians have been heard in public
meeting to boast, that in their institutions the library
committees never meet, with the result that they have
complete control of funds and freedom of action. In
reply it may be said that such isolation of the librarian seems on any broad view of the situation most
regrettable, and that of all tasks calling for active cooperation between the librarian and the faculty, book
selection is the most obvious. The librarian's role is
not an ignominious one. Aside from active selection
in certain fields such as bibliography and reference, it
is his duty to direct the total processes of book selection along sound lines. This means not only assuring
the fair and effective use of general or unallocated
funds, but endeavoring to formulate general policies
and standards for book selection in all fields. These
he will probably discover cannot be rigidly enforced,
but by clear enunciation and pressure in the right
direction, a generally consistent policy can be estab-

lished and the level of book buying raised. The fact
that a department of instruction has a more or less
expert knowledge of a subject field is no guarantee,
unfortunately, that its choice of books to be bought
will be carefully made. Too often the selection is hur-
riedly done and haphazard if not capricious. It is at
this point that the librarian is called to exercise a
tactful leadership. Though he will utilize to the fullest the specialized knowledge of the faculty in select-
ing specific titles, he will need to warn them of certain well known pitfalls and to keep to the fore the
long range interests of the library which are likely to
be neglected. Among the questions which call for his
guidance and leadership are the following:

1. Should the library buy textbooks? The function
of textbooks is not to contribute to knowledge but to
summarize the generally accepted knowledge of the
field. Being summaries, they usually suffer from the
dullness which comes from an excess of generalities.
They quickly become out of date. If a library will
keep them long enough they may become of historical
value, but few college libraries will need to duplicate
the textbook collections of the larger teachers colleges and some universities. Yet in spite of this poor
return from the investment, libraries continue to acquire hundreds of textbooks, most of which after a
short period remain untouched on the shelves. The
problem is made more serious by the fact that this
type of material is often bought in multiple copies
for purposes of required reading. One of the librarian's contributions to book selection will be to endeavor to build up a sentiment against the purchase
of textbooks with library funds. Lawrence College,
under the leadership of President Wriston, adopted a
rule against such purchases. Such a regulation can be
enforced only by a strong and virtually unanimous
sentiment against it on the part of faculty and administration. In another institution the ruling has been

adopted that the burden of proof for such purchases, particularly if multiple copies are requested, must rest on the instructor asking for them, and that he must be able to demonstrate, among other things, that the class involved had already expended a reasonable amount of money for their textbooks. Whether it is best to have a regulation to which exceptions will be made or to attempt to use more or less strong pressure against this type of material is merely a matter of degree, and will probably be determined by the extent of the scholarly interests of the faculty. Certainly the librarian's task in connection with this kind of book buying is clear: He must convince first his committee and, with their aid, the faculty and administration that in buying books of this sort the college will get less for its money than for most other purchases.

2. A second problem concerns rare books or collectors' items. These are books in which historical or sentimental associations have given a fictitious or at least an extraneous value to the volumes. The usual conception of a distinguished library is one with many first editions and collectors' items. This rare book tradition is deeply entrenched, and the librarian who does not repeat its shibboleths will have trouble on his hands. Yet a college library—should one not add a university library as well?—is a collection of books acquired for the purposes of teaching and study. It is not a museum, nor is it a special collection like the Morgan or Huntington libraries. So long as funds are badly needed for the less newsworthy but more practical necessities of the library, it would seem that the purchase of rarities should be steadfastly refused.

Microphotography here is an obvious aid. When scholarly purposes can be served by a microfilm at a cost of from fifty cents to five dollars, should not college libraries as a regular policy secure these reproductions in place of bidding competitively for the rare originals? No one denies the delight of book lovers at the possession of a rare original, nor the greater ease with which it can be used, nor can one deny that in many cases the original has advantages for scholarly work. The matter is merely one of the most effective use of library funds. Fortunately, many colleges have friends who, being perspicacious as well as generous, see quite well that such a policy is merely a moralizing of necessity, and reward this display of virtue by gifts of rare and beautiful volumes. No matter how clearly the matter is agreed to in principle, there will be a few people on every faculty who will never be convinced that particular opportunities should be passed up. The only answer is to make the matter one of general policy. Both in enforcing this and in making exceptions to it, the librarian will find the library committee a most valuable aid and support.

3. Should the college library purchase fiction, detective stories and other current or recreational items unrelated to any course of instruction? This is one of the thorniest of the problems of book selection. On the question one usually finds one group of faculty members arrayed over against the librarian supported by other members of the faculty and especially by faculty wives. The argument against this material can be stated both positively and negatively. The college asks undergraduates to give four years of their time to prosecuting the studies which it recommends as a preparation for adult living. If these studies are taken seriously there will be little time for outside reading, for any one of the usual subjects of the curriculum could take up the full time of an enthusiastic student. As already remarked, recreational reading is of less importance on a college campus where the day's work consists more of reading than in other walks of life. The college library, it can be urged, needs to take its own task more seriously, not to attempt the role of

the public library, the great concern of which with recreational reading is itself questionable. No one objects to recreational reading, but should funds be taken from the serious concerns of the college to provide it?

With these arguments there is undoubtedly much of pungent truth. Yet the rigorous exclusion of all literature except that related to courses would be to make two assumptions neither of which the liberal arts college would be willing to make. The first is that the courses of study are the ideal or perfect solution to the problem of education. Not only do we know too well the compromises and practical considerations which often enter into the making of such programs but there are also the eternally unpredictable character and interests of individual students which make any course of study a poor fit for some minds. The extracurricular volumes in the library supplement to some extent the never quite perfect recommendations of those who direct the courses of systematic study. As one librarian stated it to the writer, "I've seen too many students who got an education from the books they read on their own initiative, not to believe to the fullest in general or extracurricular reading." Nor would the liberal college want to insist that all education is secured in the classroom. American colleges throughout their history have placed much emphasis on the value of the association of students together and the normal processes of growth in an environment favorable to character and mental development. One element in this will certainly be the availability of the best books of current interest.

But there are few colleges where there is the likelihood of neglect along these lines. There is more likely to be danger of too much concern with the contemporary and ephemeral to the neglect of the books of lasting value. The pressure of publishers' advertising and current discussion loads the balance in favor of current books. Rigid selection is certainly necessary, a selection which can probably be enforced more easily by appropriating a very limited sum of money to be spent for this purpose than by attempting to determine which current books are educationally desirable. Some institutions go further than this. One of the leading university libraries has a rule that no fiction is to be bought until it is two years old, the argument being made that even if permanently valuable the books are worn out in the first rush of their popularity, and that selection of that which is desired can best be made after two years' testing. So far as purely recreational reading is concerned, a rental library of fiction operated by the bookstore is perhaps the best way to supply the demand.

4. The converse of the above problem is that of research materials. To what extent should the college library purchase these? Certainly the thesis that research is a function of a university and not of a college cannot be admitted, since investigation and inquiry are essential for any faculty if it is not to become stale. On the other hand, research collections are enormously expensive, both to secure, to catalog and to house. Most colleges are under the necessity of some limitation in this respect.

This problem is mitigated somewhat by the generous interlibrary loan policy of most large libraries, by the production of numerous bibliographic aids for locating needed volumes, and by the development of microphotography. These, however, do not solve the problem. Nor is there any other easy solution to it. It is possible, however, for a library with limited funds to develop an intelligible and consistent policy with respect to this type of material. Into such a policy the following considerations will probably enter.

In the first place, full support should be given to the strong movement under way looking toward the avoidance of the expensive duplication of research collections already built up in nearby institutions. Cooperation among libraries in this direction is with us to stay, and much is being done to inform academic communities of the book holdings which are easily accessible in other libraries. Librarians have led the way in this, and they are far ahead of their colleagues on the faculty in their appreciation of the importance of this correlation. The first step therefore in meeting the problem of research materials is to become familiar with the book assets near at hand, and to insist steadily on the use of these materials rather than the repurchase of them in the college library.

In the second place it is practical and fair to make a distinction between research materials which will serve a number of readers and those which will be used almost entirely by one individual. A request for special materials dealing with the United States census might be granted, while a similar request for books on Sumerian cuneiform writing might well be refused on the ground that no one else would ever use them. The general principle here is not as unfair as it might seem. It means simply that a great many research projects call for those basic books—source collections, statistical data, etc.— which should be in a good library in any case. Such materials should be secured as far as funds permit. Books which will be used by only one individual are in a different category, and are a questionable acquisition for college libraries unless funds are available for the specific support of research projects. It is the librarian's responsibility to build up the library, guiding the expenditures of the book funds as far as he can, to achieve the most valuable collection possible for the entire community.

This leads to the recognition of the fact that the interests of students and the research interests of faculty members are not nearly so far apart as is often supposed. If routine purchases can be directed into the basic literary and historical sources instead of the annual output of popular treatises, textbooks and discussions, so much of which is highly repetitious and quickly ceases to be of interest, the basis for research needs will have been laid and the tools for first rate teaching provided at the same time.

5. In addition to endeavoring to establish general policies with reference to the above types of material, can anything be done by the library administration to improve the quality of the routine book selections in departmental fields? The answer is, Not very much. The quality of the books recommended for purchase will reflect rather closely the scholarly level of the members of the department. But there are certain procedures which will help. These must be positive rather than negative, for though it can be maintained that the librarian should have the right to refuse to order useless books, in actual practice he can exercise this right chiefly in the case of duplication which appears unnecessary or of some more extreme departure from the book buying policy of the institution. Occasionally he can with profit hold up orders of books which appear to him worthless, and ask the instructors recommending them to show cause why the volume should be bought, but he is always at a disadvantage in such discussions. The librarian's best contribution will be positive rather than negative. While faculty members may be presumed to know which are good books in their respective fields, they cannot always be counted on to base their choices on a wide enough range. In various ways the librarian can widen the field of choice, and can provide in some cases more accurate information concerning books considered. Mr. Danton, librarian of Temple University, adopted the practice of sending titles regularly to the departments as suggestions for purchase. These were obtained from book review sections of current periodicals. This practice would seem to be useful primarily in the case of those departments which the

librarian knows to be indifferent, slow, or uninformed.[4] Books are sometimes ordered by faculty
members on the basis of titles or descriptions in the
publishers' catalogs. This may be due to very good
motives, the fact that the individual is working on a
research project or teaching a subject on which the
new volume seems to bear directly. The book, when
it arrives, is found to have been misleadingly described, or is a superficial and useless treatment. The
difficulty can be avoided by expanding considerably
the practice of ordering books on approval. Book
sellers are quite willing to do this. One medical school
library can be cited which does all of its buying on
this basis, and no book is added to the shelves until
it has actually been examined by an expert. Such an
extension of the procedure seems unnecessary for the
liberal arts college and would greatly increase the
details of acquisition, but there is no reason why the
device should not be employed in all cases of uncertainty. Perhaps the best plan would be to print on the
order or request card used by faculty members the
question, "Do you wish to examine the above volume
before purchasing?" This would take care of cases
of actual doubt.

More important than these devices is the necessity
of developing a sentiment against buying books too
quickly. The policy of one institution of not buying
fiction until it had been out two years was mentioned
above. There is probably quite as much buncombe
published in the fields of the social sciences as in that
of fiction. A general policy of waiting on new books
for a period, certainly until after the appearance of
reviews in the technical journals, will in most cases
be profitable. It is always easier to buy the new books.

[4]Mr. Danton reports that in the three departments in which he carried this out, all being fields in which publishing was heavy, 34 per
cent, 39 per cent, and 46 per cent of the ordering was of titles suggested. J. P. Danton, "The Faculty, the Librarian and Book Selection," *Library Journal*, LXI (1936), 715-17.

Going back requires care, competence in the field, and a balanced judgment. But for most small and growing libraries it would seem scarcely debatable that most of their book acquisitions should be selected from those of volumes which have stood the test of time and represent the real literary and scientific achievements of our culture. Mr. Randall in his volume *The College Library,* which rests on a survey of many libraries, reports that "a formal plan for developing the book collection is almost never to be found."[5]

There are several ways in which the librarian can forward this process of careful consideration of important volumes which may not be under current discussion and hence overlooked at the moment of ordering. The most important is probably that of checking the library's holdings against the standard bibliographies and check lists, and reporting to the department the titles which the library does not possess. Much time will be saved and personal relations made smoother if this is done by previous arrangement and agreement. Enlightened by this information, the department will be far down the road toward a careful and intelligent development of its book resources.

A second line of action looking toward the same end can be followed in the use of unallocated funds, that is, those held at the discretion of the librarian with the advice of his committee. Appropriations supplementing the regular departmental funds can be awarded to those departments or groups which have given evidence of a systematic survey of their holdings and needs and a careful plan for the development of the field. It may be that the librarian will have to initiate such proposals in their broad outline to departments which are weak and uninterested.

In all of this discussion it has been the college with

[5]William M. Randall, *The College Library* (Chicago: American Library Association and University of Chicago Press, 1932), p.21ff.

limited book funds with which we have been concerned. As the book collection grows larger and as funds become more ample, a definite change comes into the problem of book selection. The faculties are certainly as competent as in the smaller schools, but their sense of book need is less, and the burden of making out requisition cards for the larger amounts available for expenditure is heavier. Book selection becomes more of a chore. Coordinate with these developments is an increase in the library staff, and the possibility of adding to it subject specialists in a number of fields of knowedge. This means that in the larger universities the responsibility for book selection will devolve more and more upon the library. The situation would seem to call for the allocation of certain fields to different members of the staff who would work in cooperation with and to a certain extent under the direction of the departmental faculties. The Librarian of Harvard University has recently raised the question whether book selection may not be better done by one with less knowledge who does the job with more thoroughness and care, than by experts who give it hurried attention. A number of larger libraries now have on their staffs individuals holding the Ph.D. degree in subject fields and there seems no reason why they should not take over to a greater or less degree the detailed but important work of book acquisition.

This rather lengthy discussion can be summarized in brief terms. In most colleges the selection of books to be bought in the various fields of specialization will of necessity be done by the faculty. For the most successful performance of this work a regular sum should be available to encourage planning of purchases and to stabilize routines. In addition other funds should be in the hands of the central administrative forces to supplement departmental programs, and to care for interdepartmental and general needs.

In the selection of larger items to be bought and in the general handling of these central funds the librarian should not act alone, but with the advice of a library committee composed chiefly of faculty members. The librarian's duties are not so much those of actual selection, save in quite limited fields, but of the direction and guidance of the whole program. Being ultimately responsible he must have the final authority in all matters of buying, but as a wise man he will recognize the limitations of his own knowledge and make the fullest use of the specialized skills of the faculty. His task is thus one of leadership and of service. His influence must always be on the side of the acquisition of books of permanent value, which means that in addition to being an efficient and tactful administrator, he must be a scholar in instinct, and thoroughly aware of what is fundamental in the process of education.

CHAPTER ELEVEN

Bridging the Gap

THE THESIS RUNNING THROUGH THIS VOLUME HAS BEEN that the primary task of the college library is to provide certain facilities for and to aid in carrying out the instructional program of the faculty. Other functions such as the provision of reading materials along non-curricula lines and even of books for faculty research, though desirable and important are secondary to this main task. Yet for reasons which have been discussed, the program of the library and that of the faculty have not been a unit. There has been lacking a sense of common purpose and, consequently, attention to the problem of the most effective coordination of effort.

Librarians are aware of this lack of integration, though the aspects of it which loom largest are, naturally enough, the difference in status and rank between members of the faculty on the one hand and the library staff on the other. They would like to see the "gap," as it is often called, bridged, and would go to almost any lengths toward that end. The matter, however, is not one merely of good-will. It involves certain administrative steps directed toward uniting the efforts of instructors and librarians so that the educational program will function as a single unit. It involves also modifications, in emphasis at least, in the program of many libraries, and a greater concern for student reading and interest in library matters on the part of many faculties.

Some of the emphases and arrangements which will

contribute to this integration of effort have already been mentioned, and there are others of which one can speak with fair confidence. The problem ranges out, however, into an area in which only the most tentative steps have been taken and in which there is no authoritative word to be given. In what follows it will be impossible to stay completely within the realm of the tried and proven, but experienced administrators do not need to be warned that all such suggestions of an administrative character, like theological doctrines, have to be applied by the sinner to his own condition.

The first step is one about which there can be little question. If the library is to function intelligently as part of the educational program, the librarian must be placed in a position in which he will be informed as to what is going on. In practical terms this means in most institutions changing the status of the librarian. In a great many colleges and universities they are not even members of the faculty, whose educational objectives they are expected to carry out.

This point has already been discussed and it is not necessary to repeat the arguments which were given for bringing the college librarian more closely into the area of educational discussion. Nor is it necessary to say again that the mere title "professor" has no sacramental efficacy. The problem is one of achieving for the librarian, *qua* librarian, an organizational position corresponding to the centrality of his responsibilities. The values resulting from such arrangements will be not only a fuller cooperation with instructors in the library aspects of this work, but also a more intelligent understanding of the relation of the library to the larger issues and efforts of the institution. Of the latter a striking illustration can be given. When the Joint Committee on Intellectual Cooperation was set up by the University of North Carolina and Duke University, the responsible library officials of both institutions were made members. Through this contact with the policy forming committee, they were enabled to plan the cooperative library program which is functioning so successfully in both institutions.

The second approach to the problem of integrating library management and educational ends must come from the library side, though it will flow in part from the above steps. It consists in reworking the program of the library from the point of view that the primary concern of the library, as well as of the rest of the college, is the effectiveness of the courses of study. Too frequently even when this point of view has been accepted, it has been a passive acquiescence, rather than a positive program.

The writer recalls a conversation with a very competent and successful college librarian who had just completed a move into a new library building. The president of that college was keenly aware of the importance of the library and had increased its budget considerably. After an inspection of the attractive and well arranged building, we paused for a cup of tea in the social room. The librarian then stated her problem: "I have gotten a new building. I have two additional members of the staff, the book funds have been increased. Of course we could use additional funds and would like to have them, but no serious problem exists here. Now what do I do next?" The problem was clearly formulated and honestly faced. The familiar library program has been one of securing more and more facilities, a program which no one could deny to be essential for effective work. But if its objectives do not look beyond this, or if these further ends are conceived to be in the hands of other branches of the college, the facilities secured will always remain to a certain extent potentialities rather than active instruments of education. So far as the library itself is concerned a program conceived in terms of facilities rather than more fundamental ends is all too likely to become enthralled to its own processes and resources.

A detailed description of the program which should supplement that of acquisition and preparation, the present writer would not attempt to supply. Certain directions which it would take, however, can be seen. It certainly involves knowing more about the work being carried on in the several departments than is commonly the case. This can be secured by study of the catalog and of syllabi of courses, and by going over points of uncertainty in the latter in conferences with individual faculty members. Attendance at departmental meetings, particularly when the work of large courses is to be discussed, would be quite profitable, although this could only be done by invitation, a point which the library committee might arrange.

"What do I do next?" One can only suggest that the courses be taken up one at a time, and their objectives and library needs examined. Out of such a study would come several specific steps. Among the first would certainly be a more intelligent judgment on the subject of the number of duplicates required for various titles, a point on which the librarian can speak with more wisdom than can the faculty member. Closely related would be a modification of circulation rules which would adjust these more exactly to the reading demands of the course. A distinction between three-hour books, three-day books and seven-day books is carried out without difficulty by a number of libraries. An effective contribution along a quite different line can also be anticipated. It would consist in bringing to the attention of the class—and incidentally of the instructor—materials in the library related to the course of study. There are several ways in which this can be done. One would be by preparing a supplementary bibliography classified under several headings. Such a list—revised of course by the instructor—mimeographed and placed in student hands, would supplement and tend to broaden the instruction from which some classes at least suffer. A second approach would be to prepare small exhibits of material in the library dealing with special topics treated in the course. Library staffs are skillful at such displays—much more so than most faculty members—and there seems no reason why this skill should not be brought to the aid of important courses. A third method would be to place supplementary material, such as biographies of important figures touched in the course, on the shelf alongside the volumes containing the required readings.[1]

A third result of a fuller acquaintance with the courses and their objectives would be more adequate assistance in connection with themes and special assignments. In the first place, every step toward a freer and more active cooperation between the library staff and the teaching groups makes it easier for the former to report to the latter difficulties encountered by students in their effort to carry out these assignments. Mr. Peyton Hurt has described the fruitful results of an analysis of a number of undergraduate courses in the University of California. In a number of cases the wording of term paper assignments was changed at the suggestion of the librarian, with the result that student access to library materials was made easier and with gains both to the library and the students.[2] An even more striking illustration can be drawn from the Library of the Woman's College of

[1]The librarian who undertakes to call the attention of the class to the full resources of the library on the subject studied will meet from some instructors the objection that they do not want the class to read these additional books but only the ones specified in the outlines. The difficulty is not what to do with this objection, but what to do with such instructors. In most cases, however, no instructor will object to such efforts unless he misunderstands what is being attempted. There should be no grounds for such misunderstanding. All such steps as have been suggested should follow a discussion with the instructor and should enlist his assistance.

[2]*The University Library and Undergraduate Instruction* (Berkeley: University of California Press, 1937), p.19ff.

the University of North Carolina. One of the assignments customarily made to freshmen in this institution was a "survey theme" involving the use of material from a number of sources. Difficulties frequently arose because the subjects assigned called for material which the library did not possess. The upshot of a series of discussions was that finally the list of topics on which these themes could be written was made up by the library staff and turned over to the departmental faculty concerned.

There is one objection to all of this. It is that exhibits, book lists, conferences with instructors and like activities are all very time consuming. Who is going to do all of this? Here a proposal which may seem radical will be made. All but the smallest colleges have reference librarians whose duties are often described in very impressive general terms—"to interpret the reader to the library and the library to the reader," etc.—but whose actual work consists to a considerable extent in answering routine questions.[3] The pattern for this sort of work seems to come from the public library, where readers of all sorts need help in the use of even the more familiar reference tools, and suggestions as to books to read on a variety of subjects. On a college campus the direction of reading in general is in the hands of the faculty. A well qualified librarian who is free to deal with student questions is an obvious asset, but the definition of his or her duties has not yet been worked out in college

[3]The Reference Department of the Duke University Library kept a record of the questions asked from September 4th to April 25th of the academic year 1937-38, classifying these in two groups. Of 6,852 questions so classified—it is recognized that the record was never quite complete—68 per cent were grouped as routine questions and 32 per cent as reference questions. Similar figures for the Woman's College Library of the same institution, a smaller library with a less extensive reference collection, and therefore with fewer questions as to the location of books, etc., showed 40 per cent reference questions. This of course does not minimize the value of the reference work done, but does suggest that a highly trained librarian will not have his or her full time and attention taken up by such questions. In the General Library referred to above these reference questions averaged about 10 per day.

terms. The suggestion is made that the college refer-ence librarian—and may we not find a better title?—should not be located in a room in the library, but a good part of the time should be outside the library building in communication with faculty members, and in some cases attending classes so as to assure the fullest cooperation of the library staff with the work of in-struction. Of such a conception of the reference librar-ian's position the distinguished work of Miss Luding-ton at Mills College can be cited in illustration. In smaller libraries this work will of course devolve upon the librarian; in the larger institutions, on the several subject specialists related to particular departments whose presence on the staff has been recommended. To the objection of lack of time one further general an-swer can be made: such efforts as have been described, undertaken only in a desire to aid the faculty in its work, will be one of the most direct ways toward get-ting the united support of the faculty for a library staff adequate for the work of the college.

In the above discussion a sort of library service has been sketched in which the librarian becomes the assistant to the instructor. There remains to be men-tioned certain developments in which the instructor is moved into the library and becomes virtually an assistant to the librarian. This development is re-lated to those changes in the form of college teach-ing which leave the student more or less free from regular class instruction, dependent upon his own labor in the library, though with faculty direction. When this takes place the problem arises of giving the student adequate guidance and assistance, some of which is provided by regularly preceptorial or tutorial meetings, but some of which is needed at unexpected times while the student is reading in the library. To a certain extent an informed reference librarian can supply this, but a number of institu-tions have grasped the problem with more vigor.

Teachers College of Columbia University some years ago experimented with the plan of placing in the philosophy of education reading room during the morning hours an assistant from the department to aid students in "questions arising from class or group discussions, or in the preparation of term papers and examinations." The experiment proved very effective.[4] They now have available in the library the full time services of two faculty members to provide assistance in any aspect of the educational literature. The "college" program of the University of Chicago calls for all freshmen or sophomores to take certain basic survey courses requiring heavy use of the library, and advisors for certain of these courses are located in the college library for most of each day. At Brown University Mr. Van Hoesen suggested that the English Department release an instructor from one course so that he might help select books for general reading and also would be present in the library at certain hours to aid students in choosing their reading materials. After a year's trial the plan was extended into "an experiment" with six library counselors from different departments, each putting in two hours a week at stated times. At Wesleyan University a member of the Classics Department has an office in the library where he is available several afternoons a week to aid students on problems involving foreign languages. The plans for the new library, or "humanistic laboratory," of Princeton University call for preceptors or other student advisors to be located in the library building, not in front offices or reading rooms, but on the several stack levels adjacent to the book collections with which they are most concerned. This plan thus calls for a physical association of the three elements in education, the student, the faculty advisor and the book collection.

[4] See Ruth Allen Casewell, "A Venture in Vitalizing Reference Reading," *School and Society*, XXX (1929), 433-36.

This same effort to find a means of integrating more closely library work and teaching efforts appears in the location in some institutions of numerous classes in the library building. In itself this is not new, the new element being the fact that whereas such locations formerly were reserved for seminars or advanced courses, in some institutions they are now being assigned to courses at the sophomore and even freshman level. All such developments point to an effort on the part of college administrators to get instructors and students to take the literature of their subjects of study much more seriously. Which of these arrangements are the more desirable, it is not necessary to say, since the particular plan which would be adopted will depend to a large extent on local policies and developments.

Thus far nothing has been said on the subject of courses on how to use the library, which constitute perhaps the most familiar answer from the library side to the problem of integrating library and classroom work. The argument made for such courses is both specific and general. In the first place, it is maintained that no student can do the best college work unless he can use the varied facilities offered by a modern library. Students coming from secondary schools are overwhelmed by the various rooms of the college library, and baffled by the very multitude of books and the size and complexity of the catalog. Of the various bibliographic aids to knowledge they are in complete ignorance. Unless they are given specific instruction on these subjects, they will go through college unable to use the facilities which the college has acquired at great expense for their use. In the second place, it is argued that such a course provides one with a technique for getting at knowledge, without which one will be at a disadvantage throughout life. The world of print nowadays is so voluminous that one must work in libraries, not with single volumes. Such courses, therefore, justify themselves as a necessary equipment of the educated citizen. A great number of libraries provide courses along this line. They vary from required courses at the freshman level to elective courses on advanced academic levels. A most powerful support for such courses has been the data published recently by Mr. Hurt and others showing that even graduate students were sadly deficient in a knowledge of library tools and techniques.[5] One writer goes so far as to recommend three required courses for college students.[6]

That many students are confused by the developments of modern libraries goes without saying. Two questions raised by the fact are more difficult to answer. One is whether or not library practice, evolved in connection with much smaller book collections, has not become too elaborate and complex. The card catalog is the point in question here. When catalogs begin to run into millions of cards, the question cannot be avoided whether or not we are trying to supply too much information by this means. To this point we shall return in the next chapter.

The second question is that of the best way by which this needed information can be supplied. The question divides into two parts: introductory information and the more advanced work in the bibliography of special subjects. Nothing could be more useless or deadly to the intellect than to memorize the names of bibliographies or other guides for which the student feels no need and has no interest. It is certainly

[5]Peyton Hurt's article, "The Need of College and University Instruction in the Use of the Library," *Library Quarterly,* IV (1934), 436-48, summarized the results of an examination on the use of the library given to 354 graduate students at the University of California and at Stanford University. He cites the following figures: 49 per cent said they often felt the need of advice in using the card catalog; 68 per cent that they needed instruction in the use of the library; and 78 per cent that such instruction would have been useful in undergraduate work.

[6]Elbridge Colby, "The Teaching Librarian," *Library Journal,* XLIX (1924), 767-73.

sound pedagogy to postpone the latter work until a need for the material is beginning to appear. To illustrate, an effort to teach freshmen the intricacies of government documents—a field incidentally in which only a small per cent of librarians are competent—is surely premature. On the assumption, then, that the freshmen are to be given only general or introductory information, how and by whom should this be given?

There is of course no one and only method, since information can often be imparted equally well by more than one means. The two most common methods—aside from an introductory tour of the library building by freshmen usually too dazed to take much in—are through some required course of the general curriculum such as English literature which gives access to all freshmen, or through classes or conferences conducted by the library staff. In favor of the latter are the arguments (a) that the instructors of subject courses are rather frequently reluctant to give up time to instruction in the use of the library, (b) that instruction by the library staff establishes contacts with students which makes them feel free subsequently to ask questions, and (c) that sometimes the faculty members do not themselves know very much about how to use the library. The objections to such courses given by the library staff are that (a) the library staff is extremely busy already, (b) that many students do not need this introductory training, and (c) that librarians, like most experts, want to teach students too much. The last point can be expanded into the general objection that all efforts of special interests to introduce into the curriculum courses dealing with methods rather than cultural content is to be opposed vigorously by those who would preserve the liberal arts tradition.

While repeating the statement that no way of doing this work of instruction is better in all cases than others, two suggestions may be made. These are complementary to each other, and should be considered together rather than separately. The first, based on the truisms that unnecessary instruction is deadly for the student and expensive for the institution, and that students vary greatly in their need for the sort of instruction under discussion, is that a test or examination be given all freshmen sometime during the academic year and that those revealing gross deficiencies be assigned to the librarian for special instruction of an introductory character. A test which may serve this purpose has recently been prepared and standardized by Miss Lulu Ruth Reed. The test has been given to students in a number of colleges and a normal score established.[7] By the use of this or some other test, those needing instruction can be determined. The library staff can then arrange small groups for instructional purposes. A certificate from the librarian that the student is qualified to go ahead might well be required. Some such plan as this is being worked out at Lawrence College where the Reed test was given to all undergraduates. It was found that while the score of the four academic classes rose with their rank, the mark of the lowest senior was below that of the lowest freshman.

The second suggestion complements the above. It is that the librarian should endeavor by various means to bring to the attention of the faculty the problem of student inability to use the library. So much of what is basically essential can be secured indirectly and in connection with other work, that even a little attention to the problem by faculty members can assure a reasonable knowledge on the students' part on all essential points.

[7]The test may be secured from the Chicago Planograph Corporation, 517 South Jefferson St., Chicago, at a cost of 4c each. At first glance one is impressed with the number of questions that no one but an expert reference librarian or cataloger could answer. Miss Reed explains that these questions are included to assure a sufficient range for the test. It is not expected that undergraduates will score 100.

This leads to the other aspect of this problem—the more advanced instruction in bibliography. Excellent courses of this sort are being given by a number of librarians, but it would seem that the general solution of the problem can be achieved only by the experts in various fields and in connection with advanced courses. That this matter is now neglected and that graduate students report themselves unfamiliar with approaches to library materials which they should know and use, is simply another piece of evidence that faculties, for all their concern for libraries for their own use, have neglected much of their teaching opportunity as regards them. That the facts justify efforts on the part of libraries to rig up courses to teach bibliography in all fields would seem very doubtful. The problem will not be solved by the assumption by the library of this part of what is properly the work of each advanced department, but by bringing to the attention of department heads the deficiency of many graduate students in this respect. If frequent and cooperative contacts are established between the library staff and the faculty, as has been suggested, information relayed by the former as to difficulties students encounter in writing term papers and other exercises will also call attention to the point. There can be no possible objection, of course, to the use of the library staff by instructors for discussions with their classes of special library problems or materials. The point which should be guarded against is the library taking over all responsibility for bibliographic instruction.

One way by which it is proposed that the gap between the library staff and the faculty be bridged has been discussed in a previous chapter. It is that librarians should teach courses in the regular departmental fields. By so doing they become not merely librarians but instructors as well. No objection to this can be raised, provided the librarian has the qualifications and the time, but it would not seem to be the basic solution of the problem. This would seem to rest on opening channels of communication, understanding and cooperation between the reading aspects of instruction and the classroom aspects rather than by combining in the person of the librarian two disparate functions. As one means toward this end the teaching of a course by the librarian might be desirable, but it is not the only way by which the end can be achieved nor in all cases the best way. The librarian, by giving formal instruction, would become closely related to one department of the college, but he would achieve thereby no similar relationship to the other departments. A second dubious approach to the general problem was revealed as such by a very wise university president to whom it was submitted. The suggestion was made that since we have in many departments of instruction assistants to read papers or to aid in research, why not a "library assistant" who would see that reserve lists were kept in order and that book orders were timed properly and other library matters attended to. "If you do that," he remarked, "the faculty members themselves might never come near the library."

In the last analysis a problem of this sort can be solved only on the campus itself. Administrators who have clearly in mind the goal to be reached will find their own way of making progress toward it.

CHAPTER TWELVE

The Costs of
Library Service

NOT ONLY WOULD IT BREAK A TIME-HONORED TRADITION to conclude a discussion of college libraries without dealing with the subject of the proper budget, but it would also ignore one of the most real of all problems connected with the library. Certainly this is the one problem which the college administrator cannot escape.

A great deal has been written and many estimates, studies and recommendations have been made of what a college should spend on its library. Although these have been collected and summarized several times, a review of certain of these will serve as an introduction to what is to follow. The following list confines itself to factual studies except in the first instance, an exception regarded as permissible because of the wide influence of the standard stated:

1. Probably the most familiar of all recommendations or standards as to the proper library budget was that which the North Central Association of Colleges and Secondary Schools maintained for some years. It called for an expenditure of at least $5 per student for the purchase of books and current periodicals. This standard was accepted and reaffirmed by several similar associations in other parts of the country. It has now been abandoned by the Association in favor of a general recommendation: "Expenditures for accessions . . . should be sufficient to cover needed replacements of and additions to the present holdings," and "expenditures for salaries of library personnel

should be sufficient to secure competent service."[1] In spite of its official abandonment, one finds that this earlier standard is still regarded with favor in some institutions.

2. A study of 14 New England colleges in 1926 showed an average annual expenditure for all library purposes of $23.69 per student, $9.39 being for books, periodicals, and binding. On a per instructor basis, the total library expenditure was $270; $105 per instructor being for books, periodicals, and binding.[2]

3. In 1928 an American Library Association committee studied the budgets of 100 colleges and universities, and on this basis prepared two recommendations which, it recommended, should be simultaneously adhered to: Expenditures for all library purposes should average $25 per student ($20 per student where the enrolment exceeded 8,000) and should be not less than 4 per cent of the total college or university budget.[3]

4. The survey of land grant colleges and universities made by the U. S. Bureau of Education in 1930 included a section on the library. This study was very carefully done and the conclusions were conservatively drawn. Among the institutions surveyed two groups clearly marked out by applying five different tests of use. One of these, "libraries with small use," showed average library expenditures of less than eleven dollars per student. "Libraries with use well above the average" had expenditures of more than twenty dollars per student. In the final summary the following recommendation was made: "Institutions which are allotting less than four per cent of their funds for library purposes or which are spending less

[1]Douglas Waples, *et al.*, *The Library* ("Evaluation of Higher Institutions," No. 4; Chicago: University of Chicago Press, 1936), p.2.
[2]Reported to the 1926 meeting of New England College Libraries by W. P. Lewis. *Libraries*, XXXI (1926), 356-57.
[3]A.L.A. Committee on Classification of Library Personnel, "Budget Classification and Compensation Plan for University and College Librarians" (Mimeo.; Chicago: American Library Association, 1929), p.4ff.

than twenty dollars per student should carefully examine the use made of their libraries, the adequacy of the book collections and the efficiency of the personnel as compared with libraries with larger ratios of expenditure."[4]

5. In the volume of Randall and Goodrich which has been repeatedly referred to, are cited the average expenditures for two groups of colleges.[5] One group is composed of 20 carefully selected colleges, all with enrolments of less than a thousand students, which are homogeneous in curricula and objectives, and which are judged as giving reasonably adequate library service. These colleges have on the average 83,000 volumes in their libraries, 315 current periodical subscriptions, an enrolment of 565 students, and a teaching staff of 56 instructors. The second group is one of 95 colleges representing a random sample of American colleges, from which the 20 referred to are selected. The average size of the book collection in these 95 colleges was 48,085. The first group, believed to be giving adequate service, has an average expenditure for library purposes of $16,700 per year, whereas the random sample of 95 colleges spend on the average $9,679. The figures are for 1933-34. Reduced to per student terms, these figures can be stated as follows: The group of 20 colleges spend on the average $32 per student for library purposes; the 95 colleges spend $17.42. The division of the average expenditure between books and salaries was as follows: For the 20 colleges $17.10 and $12.50 per student for salaries and books respectively; for the 95 colleges $9.45 and $6.55 per student for salaries and books respectively.[6]

6. Mr. William H. Carlson in connection with his

[4]U. S. Office of Education, *Survey of Land Grant Colleges and Universities.* Bulletin 1930, No. 9, I, Part VIII, "The Library" (Washington: Government Printing Office, 1930), p.714.
[5]W. M. Randall and F. L. Goodrich, *Principles of College Library Administration* (Chicago: A.L.A. and University of Chicago Press, 1936), chap. ix.
[6]*Ibid.,* p.218.

study of 7 western and northwestern state university libraries calculated the average expenditure of the libraries of the following 20 colleges and universities: Baylor, Dartmouth, Denver, Duke, Oberlin, Ohio State, Kansas, Michigan State, Missouri, Nebraska, North Carolina, Oklahoma, Oregon, Oregon State, Texas, Rochester, Smith, Syracuse, Vanderbilt, and Washington State. The libraries of very large universities such as California, Columbia, Michigan, and Yale were excluded. To quote his statement, "While there are some larger universities on the list, there also are six colleges and several of the institutions included which definitely do not have strong or well supported libraries." The average expenditures for this group in 1935-36 were calculated on a per faculty member basis. The average was found to be $103.54 for books and periodicals and $278.61 for all library purposes.[7] Mr. Carlson points out that this is almost identical with the average of the 14 New England libraries reported in 1926. In comparison with these figures Mr. Carlson reported for the state universities of Montana, Wyoming, South Dakota, Utah, Idaho, North Dakota, and Nevada an average expenditure of $57.22 per faculty member for books and periodicals and $179.18 for all library purposes.[8]

To the above studies of actual expenditures there have been a number of estimates of the percentage of the total educational budget which should be appropriated for library purposes. Dean Wilson of the Graduate Library School of the University of Chicago, for example, has recently stated his conviction that "less than seven per cent of the total educational budget or twenty dollars per student will not provide effective library service. Ten per cent and thirty to

[7] W. H. Carlson, *The Development and Financial Support of Seven Western and Northwestern State University Libraries* (Berkeley: University of California Press, 1938), p.47.

[8] *Ibid.*, p.45ff. On a per student basis the average expenditures of these seven institutions was $4.96 for books and periodicals and $15.45 for all library purposes.

forty dollars per student will be far better."[9] The figures supplied by the *Biennial Survey of Education* indicate that the average of all institutions reporting is, however, far below this recommendation. The per cent of the total budget in 1935-36 of 1,628 universities, colleges, professional and normal schools applied to library purposes was 4.0 per cent.[10]

It is plain that none of these figures can be taken as a final or absolute standard. Colleges with very small enrolments obviously cannot adopt a per student figure. Similarly, a percentage of the total income has no meaning as a measure of adequacy where the college has to operate on very meager sums. The best single measure is probably to be stated in terms of so much per faculty member, since this measure reflects fairly accurately the extent of the curriculum and special subject interests of the institution, as well as the size of the student body. The difficulties, however, of all these approaches are fairly clear when subjected to any logical examination.

They are, however, very suggestive and that is all they need to be. They provide an administrator with rough measures by which he can check his budget to see if he is starving his library, or giving it a financial support which would justify him in expecting of it an unusual service.

The only basis for determining what the library budget should be is a calculation of the actual cost involved in providing effective library support for the educational program of the institution. This is far more satisfactory than any arbitrary standard. In preparing a budget based upon such a calculation, the librarian has no occasion to feel hesitant or any obligation to be modest in his demands. He is responsible for the reading aspects of the college program, an

[9]L. R. Wilson, "The Emergence of the College Library," *School and Society*, XXXIV (1931), 488.

[10]U. S. Office of Education, *Biennial Survey of Education, 1934-36*. Bulletin 1937, No. 2 (Washington: Government Printing Office, 1939), v.II, chap. iv, p.44.

obligation so vital and comprehensive as to call for no apology in the effort to see that it is adequately done. If the librarian can show a real service to the cause of education which the library could perform if funds were only available, he has an obligation to state this. He probably will receive a welcome hearing. He may not get the money, but such a recommendation is quite likely to bear fruit in subsequent years. Nine tenths of the college presidents would be grateful for such requests, for sound ideas as to how the job of education can be done better are rare things even in the college world. If really fruitful, such ideas will sometimes finance themselves. An unwillingness to go on with a routine ineffective performance, if associated with positive suggestions for improvement, will be a tonic to the president and through him to the board of regents, trustees, or others interested in the intellectual life of the institution. When the librarian proposes an improvement in the library service definitely related to educational ends, he speaks, furthermore, for every department and every professor on the campus. He will find wide support, and need not hesitate in such a case to ask for a budget which will mean even more than $25 per student or 6 or 7 per cent of the total budget.

But these statements implying a willingness on the part of administrators to increase library budgets whenever possible have to be sharply qualified in one respect to correspond to the facts. As libraries have grown in size the cost of their administration has tended to increase in geometrical rather than arithmetical proportion. A library adding regularly 20,000 volumes per year to its book collection will from time to time need additional help even though the size of the student body served remains stable. As the catalog gets larger each filing or checking operation proceeds more slowly, and as the book collection gets larger, every inventory becomes more of an undertaking.

The technical processes, in other words, gradually assume a larger and larger share of the total library budget. The evidence of this is plain enough. New libraries usually devote more than 50 per cent of their funds to book purposes. Older libraries in nearly every case require more than half their funds for their operation. This steady increase in the proportion of the funds which must be devoted to the technical side of the library has, naturally enough, made many administrators hesitant and uncertain as to increases of this character. Are these additional costs necessary? they inevitably ask. While requests for increases, the immediate educational value of which is apparent, usually will be given an attentive and careful hearing, increases for routine and technical purposes are harder to put across. Every librarian is familiar with this fact. Witness the greater difficulty in getting appropriations for staff increases in comparison with increases in the book funds.

This raises a very large and very serious problem which must be frankly stated and clearly faced by all concerned with libraries and their work. Are the technical aspects of current library practice more elaborate and expensive than is necessary for college purposes?

How much does it cost to put a book on the shelves ready for use? In recent years three or four important studies of this question have been made which are in general agreement.

1. In 1929-30 careful records were kept in the Library of the University of California of the cost of cataloging 16,650 titles, being half a year's work. The average cost of labor and supplies was 65.5 cents per title. Inclusion of the book pocket, accessioning, and marking the book added 7.1 cents per title, bringing the total to 72.6 cents per title.[11]

[11]Elinor Hand, "A Cost Survey in a University Library," *Library Journal*, LV (1930), 763-66. See also *College and Reference Library Yearbook* (Chicago: American Library Association, 1931), p.85ff.

2. In the *Library Journal,* LI (1926), 140ff., Mr. Windsor reported that the cost of cataloging the University of Illinois books "might be estimated at an average of 77 cents per volume." He gave figures for 5 unnamed libraries covering a period of 3 years, the average of the 5 being 70 cents per volume.[12]

3. Mr. Fremont Rider, librarian of Wesleyan University, developed in his institution a system of cost accounting which had been in operation three years when he published certain of its results.[13] He includes in his data the costs of administrative direction of the various library processes as well as of the direct labor costs. The published figures are for the year 1934-35. Mr. Rider found that to catalog a book—his figures were based on 14,461 volumes—costs 70 cents per volume for labor. The addition of supplies, miscellaneous overhead and estimated rental costs of building and equipment raises this to 92 cents per volume. In addition, the cost of accessioning, including in the term plating, addition of book pocket and all markings, cost 13 cents per volume for direct labor, or 19 cents with the addition of supplies and overhead and rental costs. Thus the cost of putting a volume on the shelves ready for use, cost in this library, 83 cents for labor and $1.11 including supplies, estimated costs of equipment, rental on building and miscellaneous overhead.

These studies are in substantial agreement. For purposes of comparison and also because building costs are not included in most annual budgets, we may perhaps ignore for the present Mr. Rider's more inclusive figures. Confining attention thus to labor costs only, one notes the three figures, 72 cents, 77 cents and 83 cents. It thus appears that a figure of about 75 cents

[12]I am indebted to Mr. Windsor and Mr. Trotier for supplying me with additional unpublished data on this study. The "estimate" was made by dividing the total salary costs by the number of volumes cataloged. The study covered a three-year period.

[13]Fremont Rider, "Library Cost Accounting," *Library Quarterly,* VI (1936), 331-81.

per volume is the cataloging labor cost of libraries buying books of a scholarly character. At least one library is known in which an insurance company has agreed to pay on all books covered by its policy an additional 70 cents per volume for the values added to it by cataloging.

It may be because these figures are more or less familiar that they do not seem excessive. Unfortunately, however, such an average figure as is reached in these studies does not fully indicate the facts in the case. It needs to be supplemented by a further analysis of the cost of handling the different types of materials which are involved in these averages.

Such an analysis as this has been made by Mr. Robert A. Miller who prepared in 1936 as a doctoral dissertation in the Graduate School of Library Service in the University of Chicago a cost analysis of a test library.[14] The identity of this library was not revealed, but we are assured that its technical work was carried on in the approved manner which is taught in library schools. Only in one detail does Mr. Miller suggest that local factors may have been responsible for a cost which was not representative, namely, in cataloging new serials. The test library contained about 400,000 volumes.

For purposes of simplicity and clarity the study was confined to labor costs only. The fact that the average cataloging cost of this test library was 77 cents per volume, virtually the same average figure yielded by the other studies of cataloging costs, would seem to indicate that a detailed analysis of the factors which go to make up this average would be applicable to other libraries as well. Mr. Miller's dissertation contains many detailed studies of the elements entering into the costs of library operation, but the most important of these for the present purpose is presented

[14] A summary of this thesis appears in the *Library Quarterly*, VII (1937), 511-36.

in Table 29 on p.220 (Table XXII of the thesis or Table 5 in the published article), which summarizes the cost of cataloging in this test library. In this table costs are presented in two forms, direct cataloging labor costs and total labor costs, the latter including certain indirect charges, accessioning, preparing, marking, filing and revision of cards, cooperative cataloging, withdrawal of books, replacing old cards, removal and correcting of temporary cards, Library of Congress card work, a number of miscellaneous activities and administrative overhead, in other words, all the activities which the cataloging department carries on in connection with its work.

The significant thing to note in this table is the cost of cataloging a new book. While the average of all books is only 77 cents, this is because so many volumes are handled which have already been cataloged in part, such as new editions, duplicate copies, serials and the like. The basic cost, that of making a new title ready for use once it has reached the library, was in this test library $1.90. On a per volume rather than per title basis this was reduced to $1.385. It is to be noted further that these are labor costs only.

Mr. Miller also analyzed the cost of ordering books. He found the direct labor cost of preliminary activities, checking titles, bibliographical preparation, ordering, receiving, and the bookkeeping work to be 35.8 cents per title.[15] This compares with 20 cents per volume in Mr. Rider's analysis at Wesleyan.[16] A further and even more marked deviation between these two studies develops when one completes the totals by adding indirect labor charges. The divergence cannot be clarified from the published materials.

Corroborating these figures is a study of costs made in a highly specialized endowed library. The figures were given to the writer in confidence. On a per title

[15]R. A. Miller, "Cost Accounting for Libraries: Acquisition and Cataloging," *Library Quarterly,* VII (1937), 529.
[16]*Ibid.,* p.376.

TABLE 29

CUMULATED LABOR COSTS WITH UNIT COSTS
FOR TYPES OF CATALOGING

Type of Cataloging	No. of Units		Direct Labor Cost	Direct Labor Unit Cost		Indirect Labor Cost	Total Labor Cost	Total Labor Unit Cost	
	Per Title	Per Volume		Per Title	Per Volume			Per Title	Per Volume
New books	994	1,365	$1,174.49	$1.183	$0.860	$ 716.23	$1,890.72	$1.902	$1.385
New serials	73	399	255.54	3.500	.640	125.73	381.27	5.223	0.956
Recataloged books*	705	1,027	445.25	0.632	.433	288.19	733.44	1.040	.714
Recataloged serials	24	193	51.66	2.153	.267	25.43	77.09	3.212	.399
Short form cataloging	32	32	8.45	0.260	.260	5.65	14.10	0.441	.441
New editions	68	131	39.21	0.577	.299	46.62	85.83	1.262	.655
Added copies	...	278	29.95	.....	.108	35.32	65.27	.....	.235
Added volumes	...	1,206	166.38	.....	0.139	169.52	335.90	.....	.279
Total	...	4,631	$2,170.93	.....	$0.469	$1,412.69	$3,583.62	.....	$0.774

*Includes student recataloging.

220

basis for the year 1933 the labor costs were as follows:

Ordering	$ .90	
Cataloging	.95	
Classifying	.35	(Estimated)
Cataloging cards	.15	(Estimated on the basis of 15 multigraph cards per title)
Other work	.15	(Estimated; does not include binding cost)
Total	$2.50	

It should be remarked, however, that in this particular library the ordering seems to have been calculated on the basis of titles purchased, which with a high percentage of failures to secure items ordered, resulted in high overhead cost for this part of the work. Cataloging is also more detailed than is done in the average university library. While exact figures cannot be cited, estimates made in other libraries suggest that the figures cited by Mr. Miller for the test library are not unrepresentative.

In these figures those of the cost of acquisition are difficult to interpret, partly because of the lack of a sufficient number of studies in this area and also because of some uncertainties in the definition of what is covered by the figures reported. For the purposes of the present discussion it will be better to fix attention on the cataloging costs. According to the most carefully secured data available, the cost of placing a new title on the shelves once it has been secured, is $1.90 for labor costs alone. To this must be added the cost of supplies and equipment, as well as that of heating, lights, janitor service, and other fixed costs of operation. The total cost of making a new book available for use, once it has been acquired, in libraries of 200,000 volumes and more, disregarding building and janitor costs, seems to be about $2 per title. This expense is not due to waste or inefficiency. Mr. Miller's analysis of the details entering into these charges reveals that the total cost was due to the great number of different processes which enter into acquisition and cataloging. He was able to point out only one detail where duplication of effort seemed to be involved, namely, the checking work done first in the acquisition department and later in the cataloging department. The total costs are due, in other words, to the fact that our mechanisms and processes have become more and more elaborate.

The objection will perhaps be made that the figures cited are much too high for college libraries with smaller book collections and with fewer foreign language titles among their purchases. The objection is quite probably correct, but before accepting its consolation too fully, two facts must be remembered. The first is that the average college library, with a smaller number of periodical and serial subscriptions, has a higher percentage of new titles to be cataloged than is to be found in the university libraries. A check on the cataloging costs of the Woman's College Library of Duke University, for example, showed that its average per volume cataloging cost was virtually the same as that of the University Library, both cataloging departments being under the same direction and following the same principles. It may be that this was due in part to an inability to achieve with the small staff and smaller volume of work certain economies that were possible in the larger cataloging department. The second fact to be remembered is that most college libraries aspire to the same principles of cataloging which are in force in the larger institutions. Though they may not have so many foreign titles, very few have formulated any different conception of their cataloging task, and are prepared to engage in the same expensive type of cataloging work as the occasion arises.

In the light of these facts it would seem to be a serious question as to whether the technical processes as carried on at present have not developed to a point where they are in danger of breaking down under their own weight. With processing costs this great, book selection, except in the more obvious cases, becomes an extremely difficult matter. Gifts must be scrutinized with the greatest of care. One begins to have difficulty in justifying the addition of volumes unless one is sure that they will be used. To insist too strongly on assured use, however, tends toward a limitation of the book collection to required readings and defeats the effort to encourage individual inquiry and investigation.

Some years ago Mr. Paul N. Rice made the point that cataloging procedures should be reformed by catalogers themselves; otherwise, it would be attempted by individuals who would not be qualified to pass on what might be eliminated.[17] Catalogers, however, have great difficulty in escaping from the trammels of their own professional standards. It would seem to be a task which will have to be assumed by the librarian rather than the cataloging department. But simplification cannot be achieved overnight, and no college administrator should insist that his librarian solve immediately problems which will require the combined thought and experience of the profession as a whole.

This discussion of the matter of cost has not been brought in here because the writer has a neat solution to propose, nor merely to wave the banner of economy in the hope of gathering an enthusiastic if uninformed following. It is rather because it would seem that the above facts are closely related to the main themes of this book, namely, the need for the college library to develop a distinctive program of its own which will emphasize the educational aspects of its work. It may well be that there are some aspects of the technical program as it is carried on at present

[17]Quoted by Rider, *op. cit.*, p.333. The reference, however should read *Libraries,* XXXII (1927), 239ff.

which are not necessary for the particular tasks of the college library, and which can be modified without educational loss and with resulting economy. What these are, if any, will emerge from the common experience and discussion of the more thoughtful library leaders. With the thought, however, of directing attention to the problem and of stimulating its discussion, I propose to specify certain simplifications and economies which seem practical.

1. The first of these is unnecessary bibliographic cataloging. "The object of library service," wrote E. C. Richardson several years ago, "is to connect a reader surely and promptly with the book that he wants to use. Every thing in cataloging which is not necessary for that purpose is luxury."[18] So far as the college library is concerned, this seems scarcely debatable. Catalogs were created to inform readers what books the library possesses and where they are. Their basic purpose, in other words, is to serve as finding lists.

Nevertheless it is the approved practice to place on the catalog card not merely the indispensable information of author, title, place and date of publication, with serial relationship, if any, but also a great deal of bibliographical data which usually is not needed to identify or locate the volume. This includes the height of the volume in centimeters, the number of the pages, the number of preliminary pages, even the number of blank pages at the end, the form of the printing, if a limited edition, its number, the table of contents, notations of maps, portraits, facsimiles, and various other annotations. This elaborate description would seem to have been derived in part from the "rare book tradition." In the case of an early printed book, such as the King James edition of the English Bible, all such data would have value, for

[18]E. C. Richardson, "The Curse of Bibliographic Cataloging," *Some Aspects of Cooperative Cataloging* (New York: H. W. Wilson, 1934), p.1.

the reason that nearly every printing varied from its predecessor. The necessity for such elaborate descriptions in a college library in connection with modern printed volumes seems at least debatable. But even more influential in determining cataloging practice has been the example of the great research libraries, and in particular that of the Library of Congress. Mr. Osborn has pointed out that in Germany a distinction is recognized between scholarly libraries and popular ones with recognized differences in cataloging standards, but that in the United States there exists only the one A.L.A. code, which was drawn up to meet "the requirements of larger libraries of a scholarly character." This code is more detailed than the Prussian one, but Library of Congress standards have resulted in making American practice more elaborate still. The revision of the American code now being worked out apparently is moving in the same direction. Thus the influences at work on small college libraries have impelled them toward a standard of cataloging worked out originally for the purposes of scholarly libraries, and the college library which adheres strictly to this standard will find itself doing more elaborate cataloging than the most scholarly German libraries have found necessary.[19]

In addition to the description of the book, modern practice includes on the catalog card the full Christian names of the author, the dates of his birth and death, and the necessary data concerning coauthors, editors, and translators. The first of these is useful, particularly in the case of common surnames like Adams or Smith; the dates, where the library possesses books by two or more writers with identical names. But not infrequently these facts are extremely difficult to obtain, although usually they are not needed for finding purposes.

[19]K. D. Metcalf, "Report of the Sub-Committee on Uniform Catalog Rules," International Federation of Library Associations Publications, *Actes du Comité International,* X (1938), 60-62.

The college library stands half way between the small public library and the research library, with its connections and aspirations directed rather toward the latter. Even if a code for popular libraries should be worked out, college library cataloging will no doubt continue to follow the scholarly pattern. However, a great deal of simplification of the code can be achieved in actual practice for those cards which the library makes for itself. "Short title" cataloging for many books and "medium" cataloging for many others will result in no loss. College catalogers need more guidance in achieving this simplification, however, than their professional leaders have given them. The enthusiasm of the cataloging specialist has produced an instrument which has become refined beyond the actual needs of a great many libraries.

A second considerable economy can be achieved by the simple policy of including full Christian names, dates, and obscure bibliographical details only when this is easily accessible or when necessary for finding purposes. Where the information is elusive and expensive to secure and is not needed for purposes of identification, there seems no good reason why it should not be omitted.

What is necessary in such cases is to be clear as to the purposes of the catalog. In recent years this has become confused by the acceptance of the view that it is a major reference work and should be prepared with this in view. As such, its factual statements are of value for their own sake, and catalogers feel themselves under the obligation to spare no pains to secure information called for by the scholarly rules, such as the author's date of birth or a middle name which he may have regretted and done all he could to suppress. Thus we have reports of cataloging which in individual instances costs $5, $10 and even $30 per title.[20] Miss Mudge, writing against the background

[20] Cf. Richardson, *op. cit.,* p.5.

226

of her experience as the head of the reference department of the Columbia University Library, a department which serves hundreds of graduate students and inquirers from all over the metropolis as well, urges the conception of the catalog as a reference tool, basing her argument on the proposition, "I have yet to find any item of information called for in the rules for adequate description of the average book which some reader, of his own accord, will not make good use of."[21] In a college library recondite data will be needed less frequently, while the average library staff is less competent to engage in the studies necessary. It would seem wiser in such cases for such information to be sought when the need for it arises, using the economies achieved to build up the college's reference collection.[22]

2. A second approach to the problem of simplification and economy is through a restudy of the list of subject headings used in the catalog and a reduction in the number of subject cards. Many of these seem to be prepared from the standpoint of logical completeness rather than actual use. This problem seems

[21]I. G. Mudge, "Present Day Economies in Cataloging," *Catalogers' and Classifiers' Yearbook,* No. 4 (Chicago: American Library Association, 1934), p.11.

[22]Miss Mudge cites various illustrations of her thesis. A literary editor, attempting to determine the factual accuracy of a manuscript dealing with the eighteenth century in which the hero was said to have thrust a volume by a particular author into his pocket, was quickly supplied with information from the catalog as to the size of the volumes by that author printed in the period. Such inquiries, however, are certainly not frequent occurrences and the data could have been ascertained from the volumes on the shelves. Graduate students often seek portraits of the subjects of their theses and are guided to examine certain volumes by the notations "ports." and "facs." These students, however, are expected to know the literature of their particular topic, even better than the catalogers. A student cramming for an examination was observed to be memorizing the dates of English authors from the catalog cards and was thus saved the trouble of hunting through many books. Catalogs, however, can scarcely be prepared with this purpose in mind. If so, last year's examination questions on each author might be much more useful. The general principle is that there is so much classified information which is never used that it seems more practical to defer expensive processes which may not be serviceable until the occasion of need arises.

not to have been given any particular attention from the special point of view of the college library.

There seem to be three types of subject cards, the value of which in a college or university library is open to question. In the first place, it is generally admitted that research workers make very little use of these catalog guides to their professional or technical material. The reason is an obvious one: they are familiar with much better guides. It would seem therefore of questionable merit to follow a program of producing subject cards for material which is obviously of this type. The Harvard Library has for years recognized the existence of material of this sort and adjusted its cataloging practice to it. "Experience shows," Mr. Currier has explained, "that he [the research worker] will not depend upon the subject cards in the catalog. . . . This results in the free omission of subject headings for books in foreign languages, for out-of-date books, for obsolete editions and for technical treatises or abstruse subjects."[23]

The second type of subject card is exactly the opposite, namely, one of a very general character. What is the value, for example, of nearly a whole tray of cards recently examined under the subject heading, "Organic Chemistry"? There are about 500 cards set up in this particular library under this heading. All this work was not only useless, but actually harmful in slowing up all use of the catalog. The general heading has been condemned by such experts as Miss Margaret Mann, but such cards still flow into our catalogs by the thousands.

The third group is one which library practice in general has not taken sufficiently into consideration. This is on subjects on which scholarly bibliographies have been published and stand on the reference shelves of the library. Nearly two decades ago A. C.

[23]See the instructive article, by T. E. Currier, "Selective Cataloging at the Harvard Library," *Library Journal*, XLIX (1929), 673ff.

Coolidge, Director of the Harvard University Library, made the comment, "The existence of an increasing number of bibliographies diminishes the necessity for full cataloging. It almost seems as if some day cataloging would consist largely of references to bibliographies."[24] Since that statement the production of printed bibliographies has proceeded at an accelerated pace, but with no measurable effect on the average card catalog. Yet what is the value of thousands of cards prepared and filed under the various subject headings dealing with the Negro when these titles stand listed already in the 17,000 entries of Work's *Bibliography?* Neither of the two answers usually made seems to justify the repetition. One is that the printed bibliography will not contain the titles which have appeared after its publication. A reference to it for books previous to that date, however, would save much labor and provide the reader with a much more adequate knowledge of the literature. The second objection, that the reader must first look in the bibliography and then in the catalog to see if the library possesses the volume wanted is scarcely a serious one. In those cases where the objection does have weight— those frequently consulted—the bibliography can be checked every year or so and the call numbers of books possessed by the library marked in the margin. Of course the advantage of utilizing the bibliography is not merely a saving in entering subject cards, but also the greater range and accuracy of a list prepared by an expert on the subject.

Here as elsewhere the influence of the Library of Congress is very strong, and while the debt of all libraries to the national library for the preparation of catalog cards is enormous, its needs are not always those of the small library. Of these a striking illustration can be cited. The Library of Congress has re-

[24]A. C. Coolidge, "The Objects of Cataloging," *Library Journal,* XLVI (1921), 735ff.

cently completed the cataloging of the publications of the League of Nations. The volumes in this set number approximately 500. The total number of cards prepared for these volumes number approximately 14,000. The cards are a model of completeness and no doubt of accuracy. They analyze the published volumes giving cards for authors of sections. The desirability of inserting 14,000 cards into a college catalog would seem however very dubious, particularly in view of the fact that the League of Nations has published along with the printed volumes an indexed guide to their contents. In most colleges and universities, the number of readers who would make use of this elaborate apparatus would not be sufficient to justify the expansion of the catalog by some 15 or 16 trays. It may be that the wiser course would be to buy the cards, but to turn them over to the political science department as a highly specialized departmental tool. Of course the Library of Congress compels no library to buy such sets, but too many libraries feel that the complete sets of cards are essential for professional competence, even if the expenditure involves curtailing other aspects of their service which are more vital for their readers.

There is one special advantage which the college library has, of which it has never made the fullest use. The public library is dependent upon its own staff for all the assistance it gives its readers; the college employs scores or hundreds of specialists, one of whose duties is to guide readers to the best literature on the subjects of their respective specialization. On the university campus the faculty is perhaps too large and too scattered to make it practical for the library to attempt to utilize its erudition in the aid of readers. But though I have never seen a card of the sort, I see no logical or practical reason why in a college library it should not be possible to insert under the proper subject heading a card which would read something like this: "For suggestions [or, further suggestions] as to books on this topic consult Professor Adams in Room 25, Founders Hall. His general office hours are Monday, Wednesday and Friday from 10:00 to 12:00." Such cards would have to be corrected repeatedly, and the whole series traced and reviewed from time to time, but this would not be impossible. Such an arrangement would be only one of many devices by which the college might make more fully available its intellectual resources. If college teaching continues to shift more responsibility to the individual student, such information as to the help which is available on the campus to those who wish it will become increasingly useful.

3. A third suggestion for meeting and to some extent offsetting the mounting cost of the technical side of library administration is that there are certain classes of material which might be left without or with very limited cataloging. Three of these can be designated. One is that of public documents, which with the multiplication of agencies under the New Deal threatens to engulf those libraries which undertake to preserve their messages to the public. A number of libraries have been able to operate very satisfactorily by depending primarily upon a consistent arrangement of these on the shelves. "Separates," that is, monographs which can be handled as ordinary books, may or may not be treated differently. Such a handling of documents necessitates a servicing of them by a member of the staff, but open shelf use of this material can lay little claim to stimulating reading. The second class of material referred to is that of dissertations. These first exercises in scholarship are not likely to be in heavy demand. Set up on the shelves by institutions, with an author card and a card under the university heading, sometimes even without this much cataloging, they are easily available. A third type of material which need not be cataloged is constituted

by large bodies of pamphlet material of limited geo-graphical or subject character. Sometimes collections containing thousands of these come into the library's possession. Sorted into chronological or other se-quences and so preserved either in pamphlet boxes or in bindings, they can be worked by any research stu-dent who is interested in the material. No doubt full cataloging would be admirable, but it seems better to make such collections available for use without this than to have them wait years for attention or to delay the cataloging of other badly needed material.

4. A fourth source of considerable expenditure with dubious educational returns has been the quest of the perfect system of classification. This has usually been regarded as the Library of Congress plan, and the question has rarely been asked whether a system devised for the national library is likely to be the best solution for a college library. The Library of Con-gress system being a highly elaborated scheme, de-signed to bring together in one place all books on very detailed subjects, and having the prestige of a number of the largest libraries of the country, has seemed to be the mark of an efficient up-to-date li-brary. As a result, some libraries have gone into re-classification without any real necessity for the ex-penditure. This remark does not apply to those institutions where several different systems have been in operation with chaotic results, and where ofttimes many cards in the catalog have been written by hand and are illegible and incorrect. In such cases the re-working of the catalog represents an obvious neces-sity. Apart from such conditions, that the values gained by changing to the Library of Congress sys-tem justifies the major operation involved, is a point which remains to be proven. As a matter of fact, no completely satisfactory subject classification scheme can be worked out, for the simple reason that all knowledge is a unity, and any one segment is related

to various other segments depending upon the aspect of it which is in view at a particular time. Furthermore, books are not written on one subject only, but also on several subjects, and on the relationships between subjects. An attempt to put books on shelves in accordance with their subject contents can never be more than very partially successful. This has lately been demonstrated statistically in a very striking way by Miss Grace Kelley in her volume, *The Classification of Books*.[25] Miss Kelley took three definite subjects and investigated the extent to which material concerning them was to be found classified together on the shelves. The investigation was carried out both in a Dewey and a Library of Congress system. Miss Kelley draws two important conclusions from the study which deserve to be quoted in full. The first is negative:

The present study has made it evident that the important needs of serious library readers can be met but partially through classification. Searching for material on specific subjects through direct consultation of the books on the shelves is an unreliable procedure. To rely upon classification alone is far less than a half-way measure. Since librarians consider it one of their highest duties to make possible for their readers an adequate subject-approach to books they are forced to turn to other records to help achieve this end.[26]

This leads to the positive recommendation:

To arrive at the greatest usefulness for the greatest number of readers, it would seem that classification, when applied to fields of growing knowledge, should be fairly simple; that is to say, of a nature that will express gross relationships rather than the less obvious and debatable ones. Less effort should be made to place books in accordance with minute subdivisions of subject-matter which

[25]Grace Kelley, *The Classification of Books* (N.Y.: H. W. Wilson, 1937).
[26]*Ibid.,* p.127.

might tend to be of temporary value, and which, as already suggested, may conform to the needs of very few readers.[27]

Miss Kelley did not have in mind primarily college libraries in making her study, but her conclusions seem especially applicable to the smaller institutions where the gross subject groupings referred to will be less extensive and more manageable. The detailed application of the principle to classification schemes most in use calls for considerable thought and discussion. Certainly one by-product would seem to be a greater skepticism as to the existence of that will-o'the-wisp, the perfect classification system and an increased hesitancy on the part of library administrators to reclassify their collections in the hope of finding it.

5. Whatever one may think about the above suggestions, there are two avenues to reduced costs about which there can be no debate. One of these is the path of cooperation between libraries. Librarians here are far ahead of faculties and are restrained in most institutions by the reluctance of the latter to think in terms of regional instead of institutional assets. Cooperative ventures which have proven their success are too numerous to enumerate. Certain striking ones are in progress in which several libraries divide the responsibility and cost of collecting expensive materials and share them by interlibrary loans. All reasonable undertakings of this character should have the full support of administrative and other officers. The second avenue referred to is that of microphotography. This has now passed the experimental stage and no library can afford to be without a projector if not a camera for the reproduction of its own resources. We cannot see yet all the uses of microfilms but each library owes it to its readers to begin to familiarize them with their use, and to make available by means

[27]Kelley, *op. cit.*, p.59.

of films the materials which a decade ago it would have been impossible to secure.

These remarks are not put forward as solutions to the problem of cost, as will be clear to every librarian, but rather as an enumeration of some of the points at which a simplification of current procedures so far as the college library is concerned, may be effected. Each of the points discussed calls for expert discussion and definition. Discussed as formal problems in bibliography and cataloging, the above suggestions will appear as a counsel of carelessness and indifference. There are, however, more exciting problems which call for the librarian's attention than those of formal bibliography. If funds are limited and staffs are inadequate, it may be necessary to be less correct along formal lines in order to take an active part in the shift of the teaching program from reliance on formal instruction toward a greater faith in individual study.

The change which is taking place in the form of the liberal arts college, if not its spirit and goal, is giving the library something of the same central position in undergraduate work which it has occupied from the beginning in graduate and research work. Just as the librarians who built up the great university libraries had to be familiar with the materials and methods of research, so those responsible for the liberal arts college libraries are called upon now to be as familiar with the materials, methods and objectives of undergraduate teaching. That, to date, has been our weakness. A generation ago the librarians were teachers, but they knew very little about the specific problems of handling large book collections. The professional librarians who succeeded them tended to become immersed in these problems. Now that librarianship as a profession is well established, opportunity exists for a type of service that will combine the qualities of both these earlier groups.

Index

Index

Index

Parker, R. H., 25-26
Pennsylvania State College Library, 161
"Pennsylvania Study," 58
Pomona College, 99
Pratt Institute School of Library Science, 6
President of College, responsibilities, 81ff.
Princeton University, 78-79, 119, 124, 141, 203
Public documents, 231
Purdy, G. Flint, 183

Randall, W. M., 7
—— and Goodrich, F. L., 28, 132, 212
Raney, M. L., 79, 141
Rare books, purchase of, 186
Recreational literature, 187
Recreational reading, 83f.
Reed, Lula Ruth, 207f.
Reed College, 74-75, 171
Reference libraries, 10
Research materials, 189
Reserve book rooms, 57, 118ff., 127
Residential libraries, 147ff.
Rice, Paul N., 223
Richardson, C. F., 226
Richardson, E. C., 224
Rider, Fremont, 217-19, 223
Rochester, University of, 138, 213; School of Music, 137; Woman's College Library, 16, 34

St. John's College, 60
Shambaugh, Benjamin J., 142-43
Shaw, Charles B., 176-77
Smith, Donald G., 79
Smith, Leland R., 13
Smith College, 213
Snavely, Guy E., xi
Southwestern College, 65
Stagg, Lewis F., 174
Stephens College, 75-77, 100, 141-42

Sterling Memorial Library. *See* Yale University
Strohm, Adam, 90
Strowd, Anne, xi
Swarthmore College, 78, 177

Temple University, 191
Texas, University of, 26, 119, 213
Textbooks, purchase of, 185f.
Towne, J. E., 139, 162
Tulane University Library, 172

Union College, 172
United States Bureau of Education, 59
United States Office of Education, 3, 14, 214
"University A," 21ff., 25-26, 29-32, 36, 42ff.
Use of college libraries, 12ff., 169f., rate of increase, 13-14
Use of Library, educational values in, 58ff.; limitations to, 55f.; sex differences, 19, 39-40

Van Hoesen, H. B., xi, 203
Vassar College, 122-24, 164

Waples, Douglas, 17, 25, 27, 28, 64, 211
Wayne College, 183
Webb, Helmer, 172
Wesleyan University, 203, 219
West Virginia, University of, 141
White, Carl M., xi, 4, 13-15
Widener Library. *See* Harvard
Williams College, 99, 157, 163
Wilson, L. R., 214
Windsor, P. L., 217
Winsor, Justin, 59
Works, G. A., 138-39
Wriston, Henry M., xi, 69, 85, 185

Yale University, 3, 113-15, 127, 156, 159; Linonia and Brothers Room, 115

COLOPHON

This book is set in Linotype Baskerville, printed on Adena Eggshell and bound in du Pont PX smooth finish cloth. The format was designed by Harold English; the cover and title page by Elmer Loemker. Composition and presswork by The Norman Press, binding by The John F. Cuneo Co.